TOXIC LOVE DISORDER

THE MINDS JOURNAL COLLECTION

D1677962

Toxic Love Disorder

THE MINDS JOURNAL COLLECTION

Copyright © 2023 Minds Journal Pvt Ltd

ISBN: 978-81-955372-2-8

Editor-in-Chief: Linda Greyman

First Published: 2023

Printed & Published in India by:

MINDJOURNAL

Minds Journal Private Limited

Salt Lake, Kolkata, India

https://themindsjournal.com/tld

Special Thanks to Our Authors

DR. ANGEL J. STORM

BEVERLY FLAXINGTON

CHRISTY PIPER

CHRISTINA (COMMON EGO)

DOMINIQUE INKROTT

DARLENE LANCER

DR. ELINOR GREENBERG

DR. FORREST TALLEY

JESSTON WILLIAMS

DR. JOSH GRESSEL

JULIE L. HALL

DR. KRISTIN DAVIN

KIM SAEED

KAYTEE GILLIS

DR. MARIETTE JANSEN

DR. PEG O'CONNOR

SIGNE M. HEGESTAND

With Deep Appreciation

In the intricate tapestry of unraveling toxic relationships, this book stands as a collaborative effort, woven together by the invaluable contributions of many skilled and insightful authors. Each author's unique perspective and expertise have enriched the pages within, shedding light on the complexities of toxic dynamics.

We extend our heartfelt gratitude to these remarkable individuals for sharing their wisdom and experiences. Your dedication to addressing this crucial topic has been the cornerstone of this endeavor.

This book is a testament to the power of collective knowledge, and we are honored to have worked alongside such a talented group of authors.

We extend our heartfelt gratitude to the dedicated readers of The Minds Journal, whose unwavering support has been a constant source of encouragement throughout our journey. Our journey with The Minds Journal began in 2015 on Facebook, and since then, our progress has been nothing short of remarkable. We are deeply appreciative of the opportunity to impact the lives of millions through our websites and social media platforms.

To you, our cherished reader, we extend our deepest thanks for your keen interest, precious time, and the trust you've vested in Toxic Love Disorder. May this book serve as a beacon of hope for those who are struggling, and as a call to action for those who seek to create a more just and compassionate world.

Thank you for being with us on this journey.

THE MINDS JOURNAL TEAM

DEDICATION

This book is dedicated to everyone who has been 'trapped' in a toxic relationship and has survived abuse, whether as a child or as an adult. Your strength inspires me and countless others.

From The Editor's Desk

Love is intoxicating. So much so that we turn a blind eye to all the poison that seeps into the nooks and crannies of our mind, heart, body and soul, thanks to our toxic lover. We breathe in the toxicity to fill our hearts and as the darkness starts to engulf us, we slowly become suffocated. Struggling to breathe, ironically, we become addicted to this toxicity and accept what we have become - a desperate, codependent enabler in an abusive relationship.

Yet, we ignore the red flags, silence our inner voices, tell ourselves that "this is not abuse" and try harder to make the relationship work. We keep trying harder to please our abuser. To have a little mercy. A little attention. A little validation. A little love. So that we can feel worthy. We are willing to tolerate all levels of abuse just for that little bit of love.

But is it worth it? Is it worth breaking your heart over and over for it? Is it worth shattering your self-esteem? Is it worth all the anxiety, depression and trauma that haunt you for life?

No. Abuse is never worth it.

> *"A person who truly loves you will never let you go, no matter how hard the situation is."* - *Filipino Proverb*

Toxic relationships are never based in love, the thing you are so desperate for. While most of us have experienced some form of toxicity in relationships whether as a child or in adult relationships, few of us are actually aware of how toxicity and abuse have negatively affected our lives.

This book, a collaborative masterpiece crafted by experts and professionals, is for everyone and anyone. Whether you are in a toxic relationship or know someone who is trapped in one, Toxic Love Disorder has been designed as a comprehensive encyclopedia on toxic and abusive relationships.

The book allows you to take a deep dive and understand -

How a seemingly healthy relationship turns toxic
What toxic relationships consist of
What lies at the heart of toxic relationships
Why toxic individuals abuse the people they seemingly love
Why the victim chooses to love and stay with their abuser
What abuse looks like in toxic relationships
How it can affect both the abuser and the abused
How to deal with abuse and toxic patterns
How to finally fix things, if at all
What you can do to get out of a toxic relationship or help someone walk away

We deconstruct the inner core of toxic relationships & delve deep into the psychology of the abuser and the abused to help everyone overcome toxic patterns and build a healthier relationship and a happier life for themselves.

May this book be a source of comfort, guidance, and inspiration to all who read it. We hope Toxic Love Disorder is everything you expect it to be and it offers you the help you need to transform your relationships and your life.

Linda Greyman
Editor-in-Chief

12 Ways This Book Can Help You

If you are reading this book, then it is likely that you are in a relationship with, stay with, interact with or work with a toxic person. Living with a toxic person can have serious consequences and can change your life forever… for the worse. This is where this book comes in to help you end the cycle of abuse.

This book takes a step-by-step approach to empower you to transform the narrative in your life in the following ways -

1. Unveils the hidden truths of unhealthy relationships, dispelling shame and bringing clarity.
2. Reflects behaviors that have become "normal," allowing you to see realities with fresh eyes.
3. Offers a wealth of information, insights, and expert advice to navigate the complexities of toxic relationships.
4. Enables early recognition of the signs of toxicity, empowering you to take proactive steps.
5. Educates you on different forms of abuse, empowering you to set and uphold healthy boundaries.
6. Helps you identify and address codependent behaviors that may have contributed to the toxic dynamic.
7. Emphasizes effective communication in healthy relationships and teaches you how to communicate assertively.
8. Provides insights into the psychology of toxic relationships, helping you understand their attraction.
9. Equips you to recognize and address unhealthy patterns in yourself and others.
10. Helps you spot early signs of toxicity in future relationships, preventing future harm.
11. Lays out a roadmap to create and maintain healthy relationships and boundaries.

Supplies tools for healing and self-care, fostering personal growth and happiness.

CONTENTS

CHAPTER TWO
THE MERCILESS PREDATOR 79

CHAPTER THREE
THE UNSUSPECTING PREY 133

CHAPTER FOUR
THE GAME OF ABUSE 171

CHAPTER FIVE
BREAKING OUT OF THE TOXIC WEB 211

CHAPTER SIX
WINGS OF FREEDOM   **283**

AUTHORS   **329**

GLOSSARY OF TERMS   **336**

The Way Things Are

TOXIC LOVE: A DISORDER OF THE HEART

Behind the warm glow of love, hides the invisible shadow of relationships. Within the labyrinthine depths of relationships, love blooms under the guidance of trust, respect, care and sacrifices.

But the fragile beauty of a relationship can easily become disfigured when love takes a sinister guise. When promises are adorned with lies, hope can be easily replaced with wounds. And even though our soul gets ravaged by the crushing weight of lies disguised as love, we refuse to stare at the haunting truth. We refuse to let go of our hope. And we become addicted to these wounds and the pain that runs deep from our heart and into our soul.

And this addiction soon turns into a disorder of the heart. Like a moth attracted to a flame, we keep running back to those lies hoping they have turned into the warmth of love, but instead we only get burned by the venomous, toxic love. This unintentional, yet intentional, bruising and battering of our heart and soul by someone we love and trust and by ourselves is what we call "Toxic Love Disorder."

Like a silent tempest brewing within, this disorder consumes our emotional well-being, gnawing at the very fabric of our happiness. Yet, like the resilient dawn that follows the darkest night, the heart possesses an innate strength to seek solace and renewal.

> *"The devil knows many ways to abuse."* - *German Proverb*

1

Toxic Relationships: The Dark Side of Love

Remember the poisoned apple from the fairy tale Snow White? The magic red apple the Evil Queen gave to Snow White to put her to a fatal sleep? A toxic relationship is somewhat like that poison apple. It may look beautiful and tempting on the outside, but once you take a bite, it can completely ruin your life. Just as a poison apple can harm your body, a toxic relationship can harm your mind, heart, and soul.

In such a relationship, harmful and unhealthy behaviors perpetrated by one party negatively impact the physical, mental, emotional, and spiritual well-being of the other (whether it's a partner, family member, or friend). Unlike the flourishing trust and goodwill in a genuine romance, toxic bonds breed suspicion and ill will. The air is thick with negativity, and there is a constant feeling of unease. What once was a caring and comforting embrace is now a trap, binding one party into giving more than they receive.

Although you may still feel attached to that person and perhaps even love them, the joy and fulfillment in the relationship have dwindled away. As time goes on, these toxic dynamics can significantly damage the victim's mental health, self-confidence, self-esteem, and even physical well-being.

If your heart no longer sings but instead feels heavy in another's company, perhaps it is time to walk away from the swamp and seek healthier soil for your soul to flourish in once more.

> *"When a man beats a woman, it is not love but cowardice."* - Kenyan Proverb

Startling Statistics

Did You Know: Over 12 million people experience intimate partner violence each year, these statistics shed light on the widespread nature of this issue:

Psychological Abuse: A staggering 84% of victims endure psychological abuse, leaving deep emotional scars and long-lasting trauma.

Physical Abuse: Approximately 50% of victims suffer from physical abuse, subjecting them to pain and harm at the hands of their intimate partners.

Sexual Coercion: Shockingly, around 33% of victims are exposed to sexual coercion, a violation that shatters trust and autonomy.

Gendered Experiences: Both men and women face psychological aggression from intimate partners, with 48.8% of men and 48.4% of women experiencing it at least once in their lifetime.

Severe Physical Violence: Disturbingly, 24.3% of women and 13.8% of men in the US aged 18 and above have endured severe physical violence in intimate relationships, revealing the extent of the brutality.

Vulnerable Age Group: Women aged 18 to 34 are particularly susceptible to high levels of violence in intimate relationships, making them more at risk during this life stage.

Impact on Children: The cycle of violence extends to children, as 30-60% of perpetrators of intimate partner violence also abuse children within their household, perpetuating a tragic cycle of harm.

Youth Vulnerability: Shockingly, 1 in 10 high school students has been physically abused in the past year by a dating partner. While on college campuses, around 43% of women faced abusive and violent dating behaviors.

CHAPTER ONE

THE ABYSS OF TOXIC RELATIONSHIPS

UNDERSTANDING TOXIC RELATIONSHIPS

What is a Toxic Relationship?

BEVERLY D. FLAXINGTON

Most people have had familiarity with something they define as a "toxic" relationship.

"That person was toxic to me."

"It is toxic for me to be around someone like that."

We often make such comments when we encounter someone "toxic". But what makes a relationship truly "toxic"? Is there a formal definition of toxicity so you can be watchful of upcoming relationships or diagnose the ones you are in?

While most discussions revolve around toxic relationships in romantic scenarios, and with a love partner, it is important to note that toxic relationships can be with family members, co-workers and with friends too. Knowing how to identify the signs is important in all relationships.

Characteristics of a toxic relationship

In a healthy relationship, two people support one another, are happy for the other's good fortune and open to accept the other person as they are. But in a toxic relationship, dominance, aggression, insecurity, fabricated facts and self-centeredness lie at the core.

In toxic relationships, you feel pressured to do things you don't really want to. You consistently feel uncomfortable, unhappy, anxious and angry in the relationship. Your relationship is marked by abuse (physical, verbal, emotional or sexual), violence, control, lack of trust, disrespect, dishonesty and poor communication. Your self-esteem

6

plummets, your personality starts to change and your mental health is negatively affected.

In a toxic relationship, one person can be:

1. Jealous

Often the aggressor is suspicious and jealous of the victim where there is no data or information to suggest they should be.

2. Controlling and/or demanding

Telling the victim what they should do, how they should do it and with whom, and when.

3. Dishonest and/or sneaky

Lying, or shading the truth, not being open to hear things and being deceitful in communication.

4. Insulting and/or demeaning

Criticizing the victim in private or in public. Tearing the other person down, being dismissive and cruel.

5. Always taking, never "giving"

The other, non-toxic person is often the giver. It isn't "fair" support, it's one-sided. The toxic person will often be in need when you, the non-toxic person, are really the needy one in that moment.

6. Lacking confidence in self and taking it out on others

Many behaviors stem from a lack of confidence and an unhealthy sense of self. Toxic people direct this to others and take out their insecurities on their friend or partner.

7. Angry and/or distrustful of their partner and others

Some toxic people are generally mad at life. They dislike many people they come in contact with, can find fault with everyone and often act out of anger.

8.   Lacking empathy

Toxic people fail to see things from their other's perspective as they are incapable of showing understanding, empathy and compassion to others. Their lack of empathy makes them devoid of emotions.

Toxic relationships vs. Abusive relationship

It's important to note that a toxic relationship is not always an abusive relationship. Abuse can be more overt – verbal and physical. Toxicity can be more subdued. It can manifest in small ways where the non-toxic person wonders if they are noticing things correctly. For example, a toxic partner might question where you were or what you did or who you were with.

The question can seem innocuous and you might believe they are just interested in what you are doing. Once you answer, the toxic person might criticize the place you went, the friend you saw or the way in which you communicated your answer. It is often subtle and therefore harder to know you are dealing with someone who is toxic.

An abusive relationship is very difficult to deal with. Most people need to flee abusive situations wherever and whenever possible, while toxic relationships can take longer to acknowledge and sometimes, in some relationships, there are ways to "fix" a toxic relationship.

Be careful though, you can't change someone who doesn't want to be changed. You can only shift the dynamic in a toxic relationship if your partner is also willing to examine themselves and make changes.

Healthy

Open communication
Mutual respect
Mutual trust
Honesty
Equality
Supportive
Making decisions together
Economically equal
Individuality

Unhealthy / Toxic

Poor communication
Disrespectful
Lack of trust
Dishonesty
Struggle for control
Unsupportive
Decisions are criticized
Economically unequal
Lack of individuality

Abusive

Harmful communication
Mistreatment
Accusations
Blame shifting
Control & domination
Manipulative
Decisions are forced
Financial control
Isolation

Editor's Note

Can love exist in a toxic relationship?

While being in a romantic relationship can be intoxicating, there is nothing romantic about a toxic relationship. At its core, a toxic relationship, whether romantic or platonic, is about feeding the toxic person's ego and building up their feeble self-esteem in the unhealthiest ways imaginable.

It is not about love. It is ONLY about making the toxic person feel "good enough" and "worthy enough" to control another human being.

"How dare she defy me? Does she think she's better than me? I am not that

9

weak. I'll show her. I'll show her whose boss!"

This is what relationships feel like to a toxic person.

A person who loves someone cannot and will not think this way about the person they love. Toxic relationships come with conditions; love is unconditional. Toxic relationships are marred with selfishness, lies, manipulation, control, dominance and violence.

So, does love exist in toxic relationships? No, true love can't breathe in the toxicity of a relationship. While the toxic person may put on a show to convince the victim that they love them, that's not real love. It is simply a lie and deception to keep the victim from leaving.

Only when a relationship is cleansed and healed from the toxicity, and when both partners are equally willing to put in the necessary effort, can real love start to blossom.

Amelia's Story

When Amelia met Josh in college, she was completely swooned over by his confidence and charm. As they grew closer, Amelia found out Josh was abused and neglected in his childhood and has struggled through trauma while growing up. Being empathetic, Amelia was enamored of Josh and they moved in together.

But things soon started to change as Josh gradually became more unpredictable, aggressive and abusive. Josh became increasingly demanding and constantly criticized Amelia for her habits and behaviors. She was isolated from her friends & family and was falsely accused of being unfaithful. He took control over her finances and withheld money to make her more dependent on him. Confused and emotionally hurt, Amelia's confidence and self-esteem started to shatter.

As soon as Amelia recognized the signs of toxicity, she decided to break up with Josh. But when she tried to walk away, Josh pulled her back into the relationship by blaming his abusive childhood for his behaviors. He promised things would change and told Amelia how much he loved her. Sadly, things turned toxic once again real soon and the cycle of abuse repeated itself multiple times.

The above case study depicts what a toxic romantic relationship actually looks like in the real world. Toxicity in relationships aims to control the victim by manipulating them, which affects their self-confidence, self-esteem and mental health.

Being conscious of toxicity

In a toxic relationship, the person experiencing the toxicity can often find themselves struggling to figure out what's real and what's not. A toxic person can make their friends, family members or partner feel as though they are the problem, or "the crazy one" when in fact the non-toxic person is often the one trying to figure out how to minimize the toxicity.

Editor's Note

Although toxic relationships can be highly dysfunctional, it's important to acknowledge that both individuals play a role in perpetuating the toxicity. Therefore, it's crucial for individuals to reflect on their own mindset, words, behaviors, and actions to understand how they contribute to the relationship's toxicity. By doing so, victims can become more self-aware of their own insecurities and unhealthy attachment styles, which can help them break free from the cycle of toxicity and cultivate healthier relationships in the future.

What Makes a Relationship Toxic?

BEVERLY D. FLAXINGTON

In a toxic relationship one person exhibits behaviors that are not supportive and can, especially over time, tear down the other person. Toxic relationships can unfold whereby what could have appeared as a loving, supportive mate or friend then turns into someone who makes the non-toxic partner or friend feel miserable and think badly of themselves.

In most cases, people who are in toxic relationships look back and realize the toxic person was never fully supportive of them, nor were they authentic in their support – it just appeared that way.

How does a relationship become toxic?

As with many abusive relationships, the toxic person often starts out being very pleasing or pacifying, appreciative and fun to be with. They could be sexually engaging and exciting or simply seem supportive and friendly – someone you are happy to be around and someone who seems to believe in you.

Over time, the fun ceases and the person reveals a negative side you might not have seen or noticed in the beginning of the relationship. They could do things that are hurtful like embarrassing you in public, or be secretive about what they do on their phones, communicating with someone and not tell you who the person is. They can show flashes of anger over something that seems insignificant, or demand that you stay home instead of going out with your friends because the toxic person "needs" to be with you.

Editor's Note

Stages of a toxic relationship

The evolution of a toxic relationship from a seemingly healthy one is a calculated yet subtle process, involving love-bombing, silent treatment & gaslighting, that the victim is typically unaware of.

Here are the 3 main stages of a toxic relationship –

Stage 1. Glorifying
The honeymoon phase. Unaware of their toxicity.

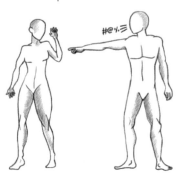

Stage 2. Devaluing
Constant doubting, manipulating & criticizing.

Stage 3: Discarding/Abandoning
Threatening to leave to gain control.

1.   Glorifying

Your partner idealizes you and believes you are perfect in every way. They appreciate your every trait, mannerism and behavior. They tell you that they are so lucky to have you and shower you with attention and positive emotions. This stage may include -

Love-bombing:

They give you excessive attention, affection & admiration to influence your thoughts and emotions and to make you dependent on them.

Forcing you to commit:

They pressurize you to commit to the relationship early on and frequently talk about long-term plans like holidays, living together or marriage.

Gaining your trust:

They only reveal their best side and make you believe they are your ideal partner and can never hurt you. They acknowledge your insecurities and build up your self-esteem.

During this stage, a toxic person will place you on a pedestal, make grand gestures of love like surprises & expensive gifts, give constant praises & compliments and make efforts to know the "real" you (only to use the information to their advantage later).

2.   Devaluing

Once they gain your trust and make you dependent, they will covertly and subtly start devaluing you. The goal of the toxic person is to break your confidence and self-esteem by using emotional abuse strategies so that you feel weak, unconfident and vulnerable.

This stage may include –

Constant criticizing:

They directly or indirectly make negative, derogatory and hurtful comments about your personality, habits, appearance, abilities and goals. They will make fun of your insecurities and regrets.

Gaslighting:

They will make you question your sanity and fill you up with self-doubt by manipulating, twisting and distorting reality, facts and truths. They will deny events and actions to make you confused.

Triangulation:

They will involve other people, including trusted family members or friends, to devalue and control you. This helps to reinforce the toxic person's sense of superiority and to isolate you.

They will constantly demand more from you and will never be happy with what you do so that you continually strive harder to seek their approval. They may say things like –

"Are you sure you want to do that?"

"Well, now I know why your mother feels so disappointed with you?"

"Why are you overreacting? This is not that big of a deal. Stop acting crazy."

3. Discarding or abandoning

If you try to set boundaries or refuse to do what they demand from you, they will threaten you with a breakup or divorce unless you do what they want. They may cheat on your multiple times with their exes or may even leave you if they find another victim to prey upon and to boost their ego.

However, in case you want to leave the relationship, they will do everything possible to keep you from leaving. They will use the same strategies they used in the "glorifying" stage, such as love-bombing.

They may make false promises that they will change and things will get "better". However, there will still be a lack of genuine apology and the toxic person will never take responsibility for their actions.

If you go back into the relationship, the cycle of abuse will restart again and things may even get "worse", instead of getting "better".

Evolution of a toxic relationship

The problem with the evolution of a toxic relationship is that you will often continue to see the good side, the side that attracted you to the person in the first place – either as a lover or a friend. As with abusive partners, toxic people aren't toxic 100% of the time.

In fact, they can be quite adept at hiding their toxicity from others. Your friends and family members might comment on how much they liked the person, or how good of a match the two of you seem to be. Yet you see glimpses or full experiences whereby you know the person has a negative shadow side you must deal with somehow.

In many cases, you might find yourself feeling drained, and unhappy but you can't quite identify why you feel this way. You want to love and respect the other person, but something prevents you from giving your "all" and doing everything to make the relationship work.

How the victim "enables" toxicity

It isn't easy to navigate a toxic relationship and while it isn't beneficial to blame the non-toxic partner, you do share some of the responsibility in allowing a toxic relationship to unfold. Many people carry childhood wounds and do not have a healthy sense of self and healthy ego to know how to set boundaries. This is a very common dynamic for the non-toxic person to allow themselves to be ignored, insulted or taken advantage of.

People who have not had a chance to grow up observing healthy relationships struggle to figure out what "healthy" looks like, so they will often provide more latitude than what the toxic partner deserves. Often called "enabling", it really is about the inability to recognize what is healthy and what is toxic and to be able to take a stand for one's self. This is why relationships start out seeming more positive and then appear to turn toxic over time.

Many times, the non-toxic partner or friend allows the small things to roll off thinking they don't want to make an issue, or don't want to be a problem themselves. This allows those small things to grow and fester and become larger issues within the relationship ultimately leading to a toxic relationship that either needs to be fixed somehow, or abandoned.

Putting the pieces together

In most cases, the early indicators were there, it just takes a long time for them to manifest and for the non-toxic person to put the pieces together and recognize the patterns. Toxic people often bring only a part of themselves to a relationship. There is often a lot the toxic person holds back.

This could be to keep the non-toxic partner or friend at a distance so the toxic person is not really known. It could be to control the other person by forcing them to figure out which pieces are authentic in the toxic person and which are not. It can be the toxic person hasn't learned how to reveal themselves in a way that allows them to feel comfortable and be trusting of their mate or friend.

Editor's Note

Although a toxic relationship can be healed and transformed into a healthy relationship, both the toxic person and the non-toxic partner, family member or friends need to work as a team and put in equal effort. Instead of enabling the toxic person, the non-toxic person must recognize toxic patterns, acknowledge and accept that the relationship is unhealthy, set strong boundaries, seek support and encourage the toxic individual to seek help.

The Dynamics of a Toxic Relationship

BEVERLY D. FLAXINGTON

The dynamics of a toxic relationship can be complex, and breaking free from them requires a deep understanding of the underlying patterns as it can help us heal and grow.

Editor's Note

What is a relationship dynamic?

The repeated and predictable patterns of behavior among people in a romantic or platonic relationship are regarded as relationship dynamics. The dynamics two people share can determine everything that takes place in the relationship. It is exhibited through –

- How you communicate, interact and relate to your loved one?

- What you think and how we feel about them?

- What they think and how they feel about you?

- How close and intimate your relationship is?

Do you bring out the best in one another? Or does your relationship promote toxicity? Is your relationship trapped in an endless loop of arguments and reconciliations?

There are so many subtle and not-so-subtle behaviors wherein you will ultimately recognize you are experiencing a toxic relationship.

Is your relationship toxic?

Let's look at a number of dynamics that can occur to assess whether your relationship is toxic or not-

1. The giver and the taker

It is said in life there are takers, and there are givers. In the best relationships each person plays each role at different points in time. In a toxic relationship you will find yourself almost always being the giver while the toxic person takes. You will notice this because over time your energy will diminish to try and help, give and support.

2. Energy drain

Speaking of energy, in a toxic relationship you often feel drained and unable to continue to give and focus. Feeling tired. Wanting to go to bed and rest instead of dealing with the other person. Giving up things you enjoy because you just don't have the energy. These can all be signing the toxic person is bleeding you mentally, emotionally and even at times physically.

3. Lack of trust

You just don't trust the other person to do what's right, or to do what's in your best interest. Trust in any relationship is an imperative – this extends to romantic situations, friendships and even works relationships. Trust underpins every communication and allows people to be themselves and to be authentic. If you don't trust the other person, you aren't in a healthy relationship.

4. Walking on eggshells

You start to tiptoe around, or feel afraid of the person's emotional outbursts and anger. When you find yourself wondering what sort of mood the person will be in, whether you can bring up an issue without a defensive or angry response and you start to worry about triggering the other person's negativity, you are likely dealing with toxicity.

5. Being judged, criticized or belittled

The toxic person can even appear to be trying to help you improve; after all, healthy relationships should include positive and constructive feedback. But in a toxic relationship you feel diminished and "less than" when your partner or friend tells you what they like and don't like. A toxic person isn't trying to help you improve; they are trying to improve their status in the relationship (and in life) by tearing you down to build themselves up.

6. Narcissistic traits
The other person seems obsessed with one thing – themselves. Narcissism shows itself in all unhealthy relationships - abusive and toxic. When the person is all about their wants, their needs, their dreams, concerns, issues and what they care about at the expense of considering any of these for you, they are bringing toxicity.

7. Lack of satisfaction
You believe you are settling rather than fulfilling what you need in a relationship. When you settle, you can risk putting yourself at the mercy of the other person. After all, it's better to have someone than no one, right? Unfortunately, in a toxic relationship you settle for something that tears you down, and diminishes your self-worth. When you notice your relationship isn't the level you would hope it could be, you are likely giving up the opportunity for a real and genuine relationship.

8. Poor communication
Communication between you and the other person is strained, unpleasant or non-existent. In a toxic relationship one of the first markers of toxicity is the inability to communicate in authentic, open and trusting ways. You might find yourself hiding parts of yourself, being dishonest

in your responses or talking to others about things you simply won't share with the toxic person.

9. Success guilt

You find yourself keeping positive news and accomplishments to yourself because your partner or friend envies you and makes you feel guilty about your success. Toxic people manage to portray themselves as the better half often making the non-toxic person feel as though they don't quite measure up, while also discounting any positive wins or news or advancements the non-toxic partner or friend experiences. This makes you wonder whether you are worthy of your partner.

10. Unreliable

You can't count on the person to be there for you when you need them. Toxic people are often unreliable. You can't be too needy with a toxic partner or friend but in those moments where you really need them to support you, they often aren't there and they will let you know you are inconveniencing them.

11. Incessant negativity

You sometimes get tired of their negative views on the world – their anger, their judgment of others and their belief the world, and people in it, are wrong or bad. Toxic people have a hard time seeing the good in others; they will often find faults which allow them to believe they are superior and more worthy. Even if not directed at you, the negativity can be wearing over time.

The toxic person may mask their negativity as alignment with a religious affiliation, or political group – they are "right" while others are "wrong". If you believe similarly, you may be able to withstand the judgment but if your views on the world are different, it can be exhausting to navigate.

Editor's Note

Types of unhealthy power dynamics in a relationship

1. Demand-withdraw dynamic
Victim demands, abuser ignores

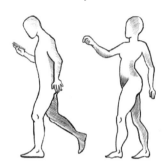

2. Distance-pursue dynamic
Victim pursues, abuser detaches

3. Fear-shame dynamic
Victim feels insecure, abuser feels ashamed & avoidant

Toxic relationships typically involve three types of unhealthy power imbalances -

1.   Demand-withdraw dynamic

Here, one person acts as the "demander" as they feel their needs are left unfulfilled. The other person acts as the "withdrawer", who ignores the requests of the partner. The "demander" is focused on seeking change and positive solutions to relationship problems. The "withdrawer" avoids the discussion and relationship issues.

2. Distance-pursue dynamic

Here, the "pursuer" is relatively more attached to the other person and more invested in the relationship. The "distancer" is relatively detached and feels smothered by the other person's need for intimacy. "The more the pursuer pursues, the more the "distancer" distances.

3. Fear-shame dynamic

This relationship dynamic is strongly based on unresolved trauma of the past of both people involved and is influenced by their emotional pain and insecurities. One person's fear, anxieties and insecurities may make the other person feel ashamed and make them avoidant.

Does toxicity disturb the equilibrium in a relationship?

When we allow someone to dominate, control & criticize us repeatedly, it completely skews the relationship dynamic and paves the way for relationship dissolution.

As the end of a relationship shatters our innate need for committed, lifelong relationships, we feel ashamed and guilty. We are filled with regret and keep blaming ourselves for the failure of the relationship. This is why numerous victims of abuse choose to stay in a toxic relationship.

But when you willingly hand over your power to your abuser, the power dynamic becomes imbalanced because we fail to set strong personal boundaries and define how we want to be treated.

What Makes a Person Toxic and Abusive?

BEVERLY D. FLAXINGTON

How does a person become toxic and/or abusive? What happens to them wherein they believe a relationship is meant to be a stomping ground for their negativity and toxicity? This is a question that has many different possible answers and it isn't the same for every person.

Roots of toxicity

In most cases, the roots of a toxic person form in childhood or due to a traumatic experience. Most toxic people did not experience anything resembling unconditional love in their youth and they carry this forward in adult relationships. They don't emotionally grow and develop wherein they have enough self-confidence and self-worth that they can put aside their own ego and focus on another person.

Foundationally, toxic people start with a void they are trying to fill by the negative behaviors they exhibit in relationships. In an illogical, non-productive and futile way they are often trying to fill the void by putting down, diminishing, or otherwise taking advantage of their partner. Of course, it doesn't work and the void only gets bigger but the toxic person hasn't learned or can't see another more effective way of being in a relationship. They strive to connect and feel whole but their behavior actually gets them the opposite result.

Editor's Note

Why someone acts toxic?

A toxic person is NOT a confident, self-assured and happy individual. They are burdened and crippled with feelings of inadequacy, unworthiness and loneliness. While they may not necessarily want to spread their toxicity to others, their inherent toxic behavior drives people away, confirming their self-perception of being unworthy and unlovable. This can make them feel even more frustrated and desperate, making them behave in more toxic ways.

They have an innate victim mindset and they believe their aggressive behavior is an act of self-defense. They believe it is better to be a predator than become a prey. Instead of adopting healthy coping strategies to deal with their inner struggles, toxic people find it easier to abuse others in order to make themselves feel better.

While it may be easy for us to think that a toxic person may have some psychological condition, toxicity is officially not recognized as a mental disorder. However, there are several underlying factors that can compel someone to exhibit toxic behavior, such as –

1. Personality Disorders

Most toxic individuals tend to suffer from personality disorders, known as Cluster B personality, that involve inappropriate and unpredictable behaviors. Cluster B disorders, a group of personality disorders which affect one's behaviors, consist of four primary disorders, namely –

- Antisocial personality disorder
- Borderline personality disorder
- Histrionic personality disorder
- Narcissistic personality disorder

These personality disorders can make the toxic person behave in an extremely dramatic, impulsive, overly emotional and aggressive way. They also tend to lack empathy, have a poor self-image, lack emotional control and are unable

to experience healthy relationships

2. Personality Traits

While it is not necessary for a toxic person to have a Cluster B personality disorder, they can still possess certain negative personality traits that can lead to toxic behaviors in relationships. They can be manipulative, exploitative, judgmental, pessimistic, selfish, controlling and aggressive. These characteristics are commonly associated with the Dark Triad personality traits, which include-

Narcissism: Entitlement, self-importance, grandiosity & lack of empathy
Machiavellian: Manipulation, exploitation, selfishness & deceitfulness
Psychopathy: Cynicism, callousness, impulsivity & antisocial behavior.
Unfortunately, people with the dark triad personality traits tend to be highly charming and achievement-oriented, and women often find men with such traits highly attractive.

3. Childhood experiences

Adverse childhood experiences like abuse, neglect, maltreatment & bullying can be a significant factor in the development of negative, toxic traits. However, a child may also develop narcissistic personality traits when they are overprotected, excessively praised and constantly pampered.

4.   Past Traumatic Experiences

Unresolved past trauma can also manifest as toxic behavior making someone seem abusive and violent. When someone has a history of abuse, unhealed grief, neglect, abandonment, or substance use or if they were raised in a dysfunctional family where domestic violence was considered "normal", the person may later show toxic traits and behaviors.

Dealing with a toxic person

While you don't want to affirm and enable the toxic person's behavior, it is important to understand the source of it. It is helpful to see the toxic person as needy and unable to express their needs in a healthy and authentic manner. You don't want to settle or be the person who is the giver to their constant taking, but you can have empathy and understanding for what could be driving the behavior.

While many toxic people don't like to self-examine and don't have the emotional intelligence to allow themselves to do so, they can respond well to someone who might be willing to look past their flaws to try and learn what's driving the negative outcomes and behaviors.

This is an important challenge to take on – it means setting boundaries for yourself while also allowing the other person to show themselves without you judging or criticizing them. It can be tempting to swoop in and identify where they are wrong or how they have hurt you or made you upset over time.

Remember their behavior is most likely coming from a place where they feel fundamentally unlovable and unworthy so it's a balance to allow them to reveal themselves without taking advantage of it as their partner or friend.

Devon's Story

Devon was a shy, yet happy-go-lucky young boy with a strict mother. While he was well taken care of, he was constantly compared with his elder brother and criticized for not being outgoing enough. Instead of nourishing his unique strengths and talents, his mother repeatedly asked him to be more like his brother, which made Devon increasingly ashamed, introverted, withdrawn and unconfident.

As he grew up, Devon struggled with anxiety, depression and personality issues. However, he worked hard on his drawbacks and eventually became a successful professional as an adult. But he constantly struggled with intimate relationships and failed to build lasting connections with anyone.

Although he was loving, caring and respectful towards his romantic partner, the moment his partner failed to meet his unrealistic expectations, he would instantly become a completely different man. He would become verbally and emotionally abusive, manipulative, critical and aggressive towards his partner. However, when his partner would apologize or make him realize that he was misunderstanding her, he would eventually switch back to his caring self and would act needy and desperate at times.

Eventually, Devon realized that his issues with his partner stemmed from a lack of love, care, approval and validation from his mother. Even the slightest rejection from his partner would trigger his past traumatic memories, making him react in a toxic, abusive manner.

The Cycle of Abuse

BEVERLY D. FLAXINGTON

The cycle of abusive behavior

Most people who abuse, and are toxic in relationships, have been abused somehow themselves. Abuse isn't always physical – it can be mental and emotional too. In fact, sometimes the worst scars are those which are unseen where the toxic person carries their abusive story forward but isn't able to share it or show it even to those who are closest to them.

People who abuse often are hurting deeply inside from a past abuse they have experienced. They believe themselves to be less valued, less important and less worthy than others. This pain can run so deep the person experiencing it isn't even aware of it without working with a therapist and uncovering where the pain resides internally.

When someone doesn't work on processing and resolving their past trauma and abuse, they will carry it forward and place the problem on the shoulders of their partner and eventually on their children. As abusers don't know how to cope with their internal conflict and emotional pain in a healthy way, they place the burden of their pain on someone they believe is inferior to them.

Editor's Note

The cycle of abuse theory

The cycle of abuse theory developed by Lenore E. Walker describes how abusive relationships involve patterns of calm, aggression and reconciliation.

This cycle primarily includes 4 distinct stages:

1. Tension building

Daily conflicts, relationship issues and misunderstandings build stress over time.

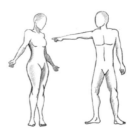

2. Incident of abuse

The abuser controls the victim through violence, aggression and psychological / verbal abuse.

3. Reconciliation

The abuser feels guilt, remorse or fear of being left alone while the victim feels disrespected, confused and responsible.

4. Calm

The abuser asks for forgiveness and shows affection to the victim. The relationship is peaceful and calm.

However, as difficulties arise again eventually, the cycle resets to the tension building stage.

Breaking the cycle of abuse

Being abused can impact an individual at very deep emotional and subconscious levels. The cycle often cannot be broken unless the person who has experienced the abuse is willing to self-reflect and work with a trained therapist to examine -

- How the abuse has affected them
- How it manifests in their relationships
- How they perpetuate the cycle

You will often see a parent, for example, being overly nasty and critical of a child for doing something they (the parent) themselves did when they were younger. For example, a father who watched his own father yell and abuse his mother for leaving the dishes to soak in the sink, could turn to his teenage daughter and say –

"No child of MINE is stupid enough to leave dirty dishes in the sink, clean them up NOW!"

Without understanding how watching abuse and experiencing abuse actually imprints experiences on the mind, and even in the heart, the person is destined to carry those imprints forward never realizing they are doing exactly what they hated observing or experiencing so much as a child.

Editor's Note

The sad reality about the cycle of abuse is that not only does it keep cropping up in repetitive patterns in your relationship, it can even be passed down to your children and future generations, when not addressed, resolved and healed. This is why it is crucial to address toxic behavior and abuse, whether with the support of friends and family or by consulting a therapist.

Warning Signs of a Toxic Relationship

KIM SAEED

Few relationships begin with anything other than politeness and pleasantness. The beginning of a relationship or "the honeymoon phase," is a challenging time to determine who a person is.

Typically, there is an intense chemistry and the flooding of feel-good biochemicals, but also a guarded attitude on both sides, trying to learn as much as possible about the other without seeming overly suspicious.

With the right person, romantic relationships can be wonderful. Choosing the wrong individual, however, can lead to years of heartbreak, the breakdown of important relationships, financial and emotional damage, and even physical harm.

The indicators of a toxic relationship

Sometimes loneliness can push us to connect quickly with people. It is generally common knowledge that we should not select a partner who appears emotionally unstable or abusive. There are, however, some individuals who are skilled at concealing their abnormal behavior and toxic personality traits.

People often don't realize when they are being subjected to relational abuse. Although most people may notice their partner has stopped being as loving as they initially were, they accept it as the natural progression of the relationship.

Even when they make valiant efforts to accommodate their partner's increasing demands, it's never enough to get back to the golden period. They may Google questions in an attempt to discover why their partner behaves as he or she does. These questions may include:

"Why does my partner ignore me?"

"Why does my partner lie to me?"

"Why does my partner give me anxiety?"

They may obsess for hours, wondering what they've done wrong and what precisely changed about them that caused their relationship to be sucked into a spiraling vortex of despair. They may become unable to function at work or, worse, barely able to function as a parent because they're immobilized by feelings of powerlessness and fear of what their partner is up to.

They may experience a consistent fear of abandonment, terrified that their relationship is on thin ice and in danger of falling into the sub-zero, deadly waters below. They begin to feel worthless, depressed, crazy, suspicious, and unable to function in their daily life.

These are signs of what's commonly known as Narcissistic Abuse Syndrome (or Narcissistic Victim Syndrome), which are strong indicators that they've entered the abyss of a toxic relationship.

Editor's Note

Signs of a toxic relationship

Any relationship can be unhealthy, toxic and abusive. While toxic relationships are most common with romantic partners, it can also be experienced with parents, siblings, relatives, friends, neighbors, coworkers, boss etc.

Not sure if your relationship is toxic or just going through a difficult phase? Here are some of the most common universal signs of toxic relationships –

1. Domination and control
2. Jealousy and envy
3. Disrespect
4. Unsupportive
5. Isolation
6. Anxiety
7. Chronic stress
8. Poor communication
9. Unmet needs
10. Lack of self-care

1.   They dominate and control you

They constantly monitor your whereabouts and react aggressively when you don't respond immediately. Their attempt to control you often becomes abusive.

2.   They are jealous and envious of you

You hide your accomplishments from your toxic partner, family member or friend as they envy you. They are jealous of you and are unable to wish you well.

3.   You feel disrespected

The words, actions and behaviors of the toxic person are planned in a way to make you feel inferior and disrespected and to break your confidence.

4.   You don't feel supported

There is a clear lack of support and encouragement. Your needs, wishes and desires are ignored and you don't feel validated or optimistic when you are around them.

5.   You feel isolated

You have increasingly lost touch with your family and friends as the toxic person keeps you isolated to control you. Alternatively, you may avoid your loved ones to avoid conflict with the toxic person.

6.   You're extremely anxious

You are extremely careful in dealing with the toxic person as you constantly keep fearing that your actions or behaviors may revoke them and make them offended and angry. You feel as if you are walking on eggshells.

7.   You are always stressed

As you are always worried about your relationship with the toxic person, you constantly feel stressed even when external factors are working in your favor.

8.   You avoid communicating with them

Instead of openly expressing your thoughts and feelings, you choose to stay quiet as every conversation is colored with criticism, sarcasm, discouragement and arguments.

9. Your needs get ignored

Even though you always make sure to meet the toxic person's needs or requirements, your needs, wishes and desires are frequently overlooked and you're forced to step out of your comfort zone.

10. You no longer care for yourself

You find it difficult to love yourself due to your fragmented self-esteem and so you struggle to practice self-care. You neglect your health, hygiene, interests and mental & emotional well-being.

Identifying warnings and red flags of an unhealthy relationship early on is crucial so that you can avoid welcoming toxicity and negativity into your life.

Why Do We Get into Toxic Relationships?

JULIE L. HALL

People with exploitive and abusive personalities are everywhere, and we all have experiences with them. We encounter them in public settings, at work or school or church, in our social circles, and perhaps in our own families. Toxic personalities are the types of people who cut off other drivers on the highway, cause scenes in restaurants, give backhanded compliments at parties, take undue credit at work, spread damaging gossip about friends and family, neglect and abuse their partners and children, and perhaps engage in physical violence and criminality.

Normalized bullying

We all have an innate ability to detect toxic behavior in others: unfairness, arrogance, lying, manipulation, aggression, and cruelty. Bullies trip our alarm system—our fight/flight response that activates to help protect us from danger. So why do some of us miss the cues and get into relationships with Cluster B types? Usually, the reason is that we have had our natural self-preserving instincts and defenses degraded because selfish and bullying behavior was normalized for us.

In childhood you may have experienced fear dynamics with your parents or other family members, assaults to your self-esteem and sense of agency, and/or ongoing violations of your interpersonal boundaries. Perhaps your parents or other caregivers were personality disordered or had other forms of mental illness that made them unable to provide an empathetic response to your dependency needs. Or maybe they struggled with addiction or other traumatic circumstances that compromised their ability to create a supportive environment for your secure development.

Whatever the reasons in your family system, relationally traumatic early experiences broke down your ability to trust yourself, recognize neglect and abuse, and set safe rules of engagement in your relationships.

The role of denial

Denial is a normal part of childhood development and an important defense against overwhelming stress and hardship. As a child you had no choice but to deny your feelings of fear and anger about the violations of trust you were subjected to. Your denial helped you survive circumstances you had no control over and shielded you from the full brunt of unmanageable emotions.

But continued denial also made you vulnerable to abusive types and set the stage for further trauma bonds in your teenage and adult relationships. As a result, you may have a history of attracting and being attracted to dominating personalities, overt or covert, who always put their feelings and needs above yours and may even enjoy manipulating and humiliating you.

Releasing shame

Many people who find themselves in an abusive relationship or with a history of being bullied at school or work, in friendships, and/or with romantic partners feel shock and shame when they begin to recognize the reality of what they have experienced. Seeing yourself as a victim of abuse may not fit at all with your sense of identity as a strong, aware person.

It is important to understand that abuse can happen to anyone, no matter how sure-footed you are in other areas of your life. Predators seek out people who can enhance them through forms of status and service. Thus, it is often the most talented, capable, and compassionate among us who are targeted.

Are Toxic Relationships Normal?

KIM SAEED

With today's social landscape of online dating sites, short-form social media trends, and the attitude of "*I want it now,*" toxic relationships are pretty common. *But common doesn't mean normal.*

While awareness of toxic relationship elements is rising, much is still overlooked and tolerated when making romantic connections, especially when Hollywood and new age theories (such as the prevalent 'twin flame' dynamic) romanticize toxicity in relationships.

Relationships aren't perfect

Everyone experiences conflict and ruptures with their partners from time to time. However, healthy relationships aim to create sustainable solutions to problems. Both parties usually own up to misdeeds and consciously try to be respectful and compassionate to one another.

However, toxic relationships are built differently. It is common for one partner to act more selfishly instead of considering the greater good of the relationship. There may be patterns of criticism, disrespect, or downright abuse.

Maybe you believe they can change. You may be hopeful, desperate, and eager to trust them as they promise things will get better. However, their words always fall flat.

That's because toxic people have a knack for manipulating situations to fulfill their own agendas. For example, they might promise to stop cheating or insist they will go to therapy with you. But they have little incentive to change their toxic behavior if they believe you won't leave.

Nonetheless, to keep you strung along, it might be that they start —

Love-bombing you - Affectionately speaking well of you and lavishing you with attention, time, and gifts.

Smearing you - Telling lies or revealing private information about your life to stack others against you.

Gaslighting you - Causing you to doubt your own reasoning.

Editor's Note

Toxic behaviors we normalize as a society

While abuse may be easy to spot, toxic behaviors in relations can be more subtle. So, we often end up wondering whether certain behaviors are actually toxic or is it all inside our head. This confusion compels us to accept and tolerate certain toxic behaviors, such as:

1. Expecting your partner to solve your problems and "fix" your life instead of simply seeking support and companionship.

2. Keeping score in the relationship and asking everything to be fair by counting who owes how many favors to the other person.

3. Believing your romantic partner to "complete" you as it leads to dominance, insecurity, jealousy and codependency.

4. Snooping around your phone or asking for the passwords to your devices or even bank account details as it is a sign of mistrust.

5. Not communicating openly about your desires and needs leading to passive aggressive behaviors, which reeks of insecurity.

6. Confusing constant conflict with intense passion but emotional roller-coaster in a relationship is simply a sign of unbalanced power dynamics, narcissism & immaturity.

7. Believing your partner to be your soul mate and expecting them to be

perfect, keeping you from accepting their flaws and making you love them conditionally.

But simply because we consider these toxic behaviors to be normal, doesn't necessarily mean that such toxic behavior patterns are healthy in any relationship.

Excusing toxicity

Change is unlikely if you're the one who's always believing in the relationship, if you're always excusing abuse, and if you look the other way or make justifications when things keep turning sideways and upside-down.

It's unlikely that your relationship will undergo any significant, positive change if you've been together for a while. Moreover, there is a downside to staying committed too long since leaving will feel more difficult.

Ultimately, toxic relationships seem so normal these days because people aren't properly vetting potential relationship partners. When red flags invariably arise, they fail to implement proper boundaries or walk away from the relationship when it's appropriate.

Editor's Note

Toxic relationships aren't normal

While an abuser or a narcissist may try to convince the victim that toxicity and abuse is "normal" in any relationship and that they "deserve" such negative behavior, it is, in fact, NOT NORMAL. Toxic relationships can never be normal due to the simple fact that it is pillared by control, dominance, manipulation and lies.

Anything that makes you afraid, anxious, stressed, depressed and traumatized constantly is toxic for you and you shouldn't accept it simply because you are made to believe that it is "normal".

Being insecure and having low self-esteem is NOT normal.

Walking on eggshells and worrying what might tick off your partner next is NOT normal.

Not being able to communicate your emotions openly and honestly is NOT normal.

Not feeling safe in a relationship is NOT normal.

While toxic behaviors can sometimes be unintentional, when it becomes a habit and turns into a pattern in a relationship, it can be damaging for you and your mental health in the long run.

If your relationship constantly makes you feel hurt and bad about yourself, then you should sit up and take notice instead of blindly accepting it.

Do not normalize unhealthy behavior patterns. Do not normalize toxicity. Do not normalize abuse. Talk to a loved one or a professional for support, if needed.

Types of
Toxic Relationships

LINDA GREYMAN

Relationships are an integral part of human life, providing a sense of connection and intimacy. However, as not all relationships are healthy, being aware of the different types of toxic relationships can help you spot the red flags early on and take steps to walk away before things get worse.

Toxicity in relationships is not always limited to intimate partner relationships. It can develop with parents, friends, relatives, romantic partners, boss, coworkers etc.

Dynamics of the most common forms of toxic relationships

1.   Toxic parents and family

One of the most destructive and suffocating types of unhealthy relationships is the one a person has with their dysfunctional family. Toxic parents or primary caregivers use maltreatment, abuse, manipulation, neglect, guilt and fear to create a toxic environment to dominate their children.

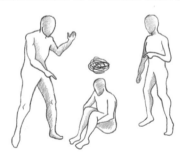

Toxic parents are more focused on their own needs than the needs of their children. Children who are raised by toxic parents have low self-esteem, experience mental health problems and neglect their own needs as adults.

Toxic relationships can also develop with other family members and close relatives like siblings, cousins, uncles, aunts etc.

2. Toxic spouse or romantic partner

Marriages and intimate relationships can easily become toxic when a partner is not supported respected or is taken for granted. In a toxic romantic relationship, one partner is always giving more than they are receiving. Their needs are avoided, they are criticized, abused and repeatedly disrespected, and they feel devalued and empty. Negative moments outnumber positive experiences and a sense of competition replaces support.

Problems are left unresolved which grow into bigger issues. Dominance, control, manipulation and infidelity distort the purity of the relationship. While the toxic partner may love-bomb the victim to manipulate them and keep them from leaving, love barely exists in the relationship. Physical, emotional, verbal, sexual and financial abuse become common and the victim is left dependent, isolated, confused and depressed.

3. Toxic friends

While good friends provide emotional support and make life more meaningful, toxic friendships are often born out of jealousy. Instead of being supportive, toxic friends are opportunists who only appear in our lives when they need something. They criticize, manipulate and emotionally hurt the victim, adversely affecting their inner peace and mental health.

They can make the victim doubt themselves by highlighting their imperfections. Their contagious negativity can make the victim feel worse about themselves and eventually make them believe that they are not good enough. Toxic friends can leave us feeling mentally and emotionally exhausted by spreading needless drama & chaos into our lives.

4. Toxic boss and coworkers

A toxic work environment may include a domineering & exploitative boss and manipulative & selfish coworkers. A toxic workplace focuses more on criticizing and punishing someone's performance than rewarding and motivating them to be more productive. Working with a toxic boss and coworkers can leave the victim feeling burnt out, frustrated, empty, detached and drained. It can also lead to mental health issues like chronic workplace stress, anxiety and depression.

Toxic managers often mistreat and demoralize their subordinates instead of guiding and developing them. They abuse their power to feed their ego which creates unnecessary drama and havoc at the workplace, affecting everyone's performance and productivity. Toxic bosses have an authoritarian leadership style and behave in a rude,

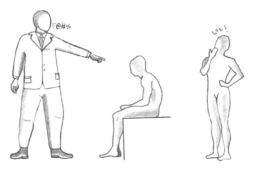

aggressive manner towards their team members.

Types of toxic relationships

A toxic relationship can occur in any type of relationship as toxicity can manifest in a variety of ways –

1. Abusive relationships

While not all toxic relationships are abusive, all abusive relationships are toxic. Abuse, whether it's physical, sexual, psychological, verbal or financial, can exist in any type of relationship.

2. Bitter relationships

Hate, spite and resentment in a relationship can slowly turn a healthy relationship toxic. When needs are left unmet, issues are left unresolved, and accountability is replaced by blame shifting, toxicity can creep up over time. Bitterness can lead to passive aggressive behavior which can pave the way for abuse.

3. Insecure-avoidant relationships

A romantic relationship can become toxic when it is defined by insecure attachment styles. While the insecure partner may seek closeness and act as the "pursuer", the avoidant partner can become overwhelmed and withdrawn and act as the "distancer". Unfortunately, the more the "distancer" withdraws, the more the "pursuer" feels insecure and dependent on their partner.

4. Rollercoaster relationships

Some romantic relationships feel like an emotional roller coaster as it is ripe with periods of emotional troughs involving disconnection and arguments followed by periods of emotional highs, such as intimacy and passion. This pattern is repeated in a cyclic manner filling the relationship up with toxicity.

5. Complacent relationships

When a relationship or a person is taken for granted, toxicity can easily fill up in the gap created between two individuals. As a relationship becomes stagnant, people involved in the relationship stop putting in effort to nourish and nurture the relationship. Sameness of the relationship can quickly deform comfort into chaos, turning surface happiness into deep-rooted issues.

6.   Narcissist-empath relationship

Narcissists often target empaths as they have a strong need for admiration and empaths can go to great lengths to meet the narcissist's needs by ignoring their own. The narcissist uses the insecurities of the empath to make themselves feel better and the empath is trapped in the toxicity by their own empathy and compassion. The more love the empath shows, the more abusive the narcissist gets.

7.   Dominant relationships

In a dominating relationship, the toxic person takes control of the other person and the relationship due to their controlling nature. They may control every aspect of the victim's life, including how they should react, what they should wear or eat etc.

8.   Enabler relationship

"Enablers" allow and motivate a loved one to continue engaging in self-destructive behaviors. The enabler often makes excuses for them, covers for them, and even hides or protects them from punitive action. This drives the other person to continue their destructive behavior patterns.

9.   Scorekeeping relationships

When a relationship becomes a scoreboard, it becomes toxic from the core. Scorekeeping can make relationships into competitions where one person "wins" and the other "loses". One can keep tabs about household chores, expenses, financial contributions etc. When the concepts of winning and losing enter a relationship, love and trust go out the window.

There can be many other patterns of toxic relationships as each individual is unique and each relationship is distinct. Understanding the different types of toxic relationships can help us take the right steps to heal ourselves and our relationships.

Children in
Toxic Relationships

KIM SAEED

Home should be a place of unconditional love, comfort, and safety. It is at home that children develop their identities, learn, and grow. In an ideal world, it should be a place where they feel supported and nurtured by their family members.

Unfortunately, home is anything but idyllic for many children. There is trouble lurking behind white picket fences, and even the most charming house can feel like a prison when the environment is toxic. In an unsafe and miserable home, children are more likely to experience adverse childhood experiences that will negatively influence them for the rest of their lives.

Innocent hearts in toxic homes

Often, children who live in toxic homes do not receive the care they require from their caregivers. And although the non-abusive parent may not realize it, they, too, are putting their children in harm's way by remaining in a toxic home environment.

This can happen in several ways, such as -

- Children witnessing one parent being mentally or physically abused (which can result in post-traumatic stress disorder or PTSD)
- Children becoming aware of one parent's infidelities (thus, forming incorrect beliefs about marriage and relationships)
- Children experiencing neglect as their non-abusive

parent spends hours a day obsessively trying to understand what toxic relationships look like

- Children seeing their non-abusive parent being angry, crying a lot, or kow-towing to the abusive parent.

Growing up with toxicity

What if the parents argue or insult one another constantly?

How does it affect a child if one parent is physically or emotionally toxic?

How might their lives be affected in a world where children are repeatedly criticized, blamed, and subjected to intense conflict?

Physical neglect is one thing (and dangerous at that!), but the toll of emotional neglect can be far more insidious. Often, parents in toxic homes are too preoccupied with addressing their own emotional needs to provide adequate support for their children.

Therefore, there is a possibility that the child will grow up feeling insecure, anxious, or even abandoned as a result. There may be a feeling of distrust toward others, and children are less likely to think that they can trust people in times of distress due to the lack of secure attachments.

Editor's Note

Adverse experiences in childhood can lead to developmental delays and a number of mental health issues in adulthood, such as -

- *Anxiety*
- *Depression*
- *Borderline personality disorder*
- *Post-traumatic stress disorder (PTSD)*
- *Emotional and mental instability*
- *Learning problems*
- *Problems relating to peers*
- *Oppositional defiant disorder*
- *Conduct disorder*
- *Aggression*

Neglect and destructive family dynamics experienced in childhood can also lead to serious physical health issues, such as diabetes and heart disease in later life. As an adult the child may also struggle with economic productivity.

How childhood abuse taints adulthood?

For children raised in toxic, dysfunctional homes, it is common to struggle in intimate relationships as well. Often, children repeat these ugly cycles in their adult lives due to these adverse childhood experiences. They commonly choose partners similar to one or more of their caretakers, and they may become abusers or abuse victims. Even though they desperately didn't want to become their parents, they are at risk of becoming exactly like their parents.

Marianne's Story

Marianne never had any privacy since childhood. Her intrusive single mother controlled every aspect of her life, from what clothes she should wear to the people she should interact with. She was told that the world is filled with "bad" people and she shouldn't trust anyone except her own mother who wants the best for her.

Understandably, such toxicity had a strong effect on young Marianne, who grew up to be detached, aloof, distrusting and doubtful of others. She barely had any friends and she refrained from socializing with others. This lack of meaningful connections, coupled with a lack of privacy took toll on Marianne as she grew up. As an adult, she struggles with building healthy intimate relationships and friendships with others as she can't help but doubt, distrust and dominate others - patterns she learned from her mother for years.

Even though she is struggling with loneliness, Marianne can't help but push people away thanks to the toxic relationship she shared with her mother as a child.

Women in Toxic / Abusive Relationships

DR. KRISTIN DAVIN

While both men and women can be victims of abuse, every time the topic comes up, by default, we think of the woman as the victim. But why? Are women easy targets? Or is that women are more tolerant of abuse simply because they want to love and be loved in return?

Women have been victims of abuse, whether physical, emotional or sexual, for ages. If you are a woman, chances are you have experienced abuse yourself and believe that it is normal of us to get treated like this in a relationship. After all, love cannot exist without pain. But love cannot exist in an abusive relationship either.

But why do women silently and willingly tolerate so much abuse on a daily basis and stay in toxic relationships longer than they should?

The mindset of women

Since ages, women have been defined by their relationships. Even today, women are raised and conditioned to work hard to keep and maintain relationships. To do whatever they must to keep the peace and to just go along with it, regardless of the cost at times. They are forced to believe that self-love and self-care is an act of selfishness and it should make them feel ashamed and guilty. Women are taught and trained to put the needs of others before their own, else they may get branded as selfish. And no woman should ever be seen as selfish.

So, women make the sacrifices and compromises in the relationships. They take the back seat and throw their unmet needs and desires out the window. They do most of the heavy lifting in relationships, even though it leaves them feeling emotionally and mentally exhausted and resentful. Yet women keep toiling in every relationship believing that if they keep working at it, things will get better. But they rarely do.

Even when they know they are trapped in a toxic relationship, women ignore the toxicity in the other person and focus only on the good traits the person has. So, in romantic relationships, when things finally start to cool down and the relationship gets better, albeit temporarily, women forget or brush off the bad times. Love can triumph over hatred, they believe. But can love truly win over toxicity and abuse?

Maybe, as long as we tolerate a little abuse. Right? But that's not how it should be. No woman should accept that this is how they should feel and how things are. Because of this mindset, women are more prone to being and staying in toxic and abusive relationships. Women are made to develop a distorted and unhealthy view of relationships. They are made to believe that relationships take constant work and compromise. The focus should be on their partner or another, forsaking their own emotional needs. Women come to expect that all relationships have ups and downs – even if they are as extreme as abuse and domestic violence.

Unfortunately, we live what we learn. Women who grew up in broken homes or dysfunctional families witnessed or experienced constant drama, abuse, arguments and fighting in their homes growing up. So, they believe that dysfunctional behaviors are normal, especially if they have witnessed abusive or toxic relationships in their childhood.

Toxicity damages emotional and mental well-being

Being in a toxic or abusive relationship damages self-worth and self-esteem. Over time, they wear the victim down. Abusers break their victims in tiny yet calculated ways, so they never see or feel it coming. Women are made to believe that they deserve to be abused or no one will want to be with them.

After a while, women start to believe their toxic partner and become convinced that they are the real problem in the relationship. Getting the strength to leave and start over feels exhausting, so abused women stay put despite all the toxicity. They just feel stuck, alone, and isolated. This is the life they are used to.

Editor's Note

Why women stay in toxic relationships?

The reason why women get into or stay in toxic relationships can vary depending on the person and the relationship. However, there are some common factors that keep women bound in a toxic relationship

1.   They have poor self-esteem

Constant abuse experienced by women in toxic relationships adversely affects their self-worth. They start believing that no one would ever want them if they left the toxic relationship.

2.   They may have savior complex

Women with the savior or messiah complex feel an intense need to "save", "rescue" and "fix" people. Due to their low self-esteem, helping others makes them feel better about themselves.

3.   They don't want to be alone

Women in toxic relationships tend to be afraid of being alone, unwanted and unloved if they leave the toxic relationship. For them, it is better to be with an abusive partner, than being with no one at all.

4.   They are stuck in patterns and routines

For women who have grown up in dysfunctional families, abuse becomes a routine and a pattern which these women continue to seek in adult relationships.

5.   They have distorted thoughts

Women believe that they deserve to be abused and that being hurt, controlled, traumatized and insulted is normal in relationships.

6.   They may not have enough finances

Financial abuse can leave women dependent on their abuser due to a lack of resources. The abuser may take control over their savings or prevent them from working, which makes leaving the relationship even more difficult.

Finding a way out

Staying in an abusive relationship can be physically, mentally, emotionally and spiritually draining to say the least. However, leaving a toxic relationship can be even more challenging for women as they typically lack the resources to live independently. This can be an even bigger challenge for married women with children.

However, this doesn't necessarily mean that there's no way out. Letting go of expectations that your toxic partner will change, finding the mental strength and determination to build a healthier life, seeking support from trusted loved ones and planning to be financially secure like getting a job, can enable you to feel more confident and walk away from all that abuse which you never deserved.

Elderly People in
Abusive Relationships

LINDA GREYMAN

When older individuals become incapable of caring for themselves due to different illnesses or simply because of old age, they are more likely to experience abuse, neglect and bullying. Unfortunately, older people are mostly abused by someone they know and trust like a partner or spouse, adult children, in-laws, grandchildren, other family members, neighbors etc. In different facilities and institutions, older people can also be abused by doctors, paid caregivers, hospital staff and health care workers.

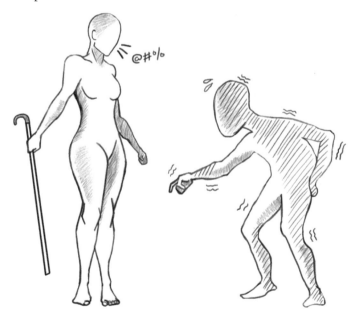

What elder abuse looks like?

Elder abuse can take different forms which may include:

1. Physical abuse

Any use of physical force that causes injury or harm to an older person, such as hitting, slapping, pushing, or restraining.

2. Emotional or psychological abuse

Any behavior that causes emotional distress or pain to an older person, such as insulting, intimidating, or threatening them.

3. Sexual abuse

Any unwanted sexual contact or attention towards an older person.

4. Neglect

When an older person is not given proper care, such as food, water, clothing, or medical attention, resulting in physical or mental harm.

5. Financial exploitation

Theft or misuse of an older person's money, property, or assets, often through deception or coercion.

6. Abandonment

When a caregiver or family member responsible for the care of an older person abandons them without arranging for appropriate care.

Elder abuse is widely prevalent as older adults depend on others for carrying out their daily activities, such as eating, bathing, wearing clothes, walking around or taking medications. Sadly, elder abuse may be hard to identify as most elderly people struggle from some physical or mental ailments which makes them vulnerable to manipulation and control.

The impact of abuse on the elderly

Long term abuse can have a series of negative consequences for the elderly, such as dementia, depression, physical injuries, disability, and inability to function properly, bedsores, stress, anxiety, loneliness, financial instability, suicidality and premature mortality.

It can also damage the emotional connection they share with their family members and loved ones leaving them feeling isolated, unloved and alone. They may blame themselves and feel guilt and shame.

Barney's Story

72-year-old Barney struggled with finances after his business shut down almost 5 years ago. Heartbroken and depressed about the failure of his business, Barney despised being dependent on his unsupportive wife Maud, 63, who verbally abused him for being "useless". While Barney wanted to help around the house with chores and with whatever little money he could earn, his old age, physical ailments and depression prevented him from being productive.

Although his son, 37-year-old Tony, provided regular financial support, living away from his parents, made it difficult for him to care for his father properly. When Tony and his family came to visit his parents, Tony noticed his father had lost a lot of weight, behaved anxiously and wore tattered & stained clothes. His father was not the happy and confident person he knew him to be. Tony suspected that his mother abused his elderly father and decided to have a talk with her to make things better.

Elder abuse mostly goes unreported

Elder abuse is a serious issue that unfortunately often goes unreported. The reasons for this are complex and varied, but it's crucial to recognize that older adults may feel ashamed, scared, or unsure about reporting abuse. This is why it's important to create a culture of support and understanding around elder abuse, and to work together as a community to prevent it from happening.

Men in Toxic / Abusive Relationships

DR. KRISTIN DAVIN

We live in a society where men are told to 'toughen up' which does men no favors. They are told not to show weakness nor be vulnerable.

"Don't express how you feel."

The silent and abused man

Unfortunately, the language around toxic and abusive relationships remains archaic at best and presumes that men are always the abuser and toxic partner. This way of thinking only reinforces this outdated pattern of thinking and reminds men that they should not speak up, leaving men feeling even more alone and suffering in silence.

Ways men are abused

Abuse doesn't discriminate based on your sex or gender. It is easy to miss the signs of abuse as a man if you are not being physically abused. You might think –

"This isn't abuse; she's just having a bad day."

"She had a bad upbringing so she is just overreacting."

But emotional and mental abuse is just as destructive as physical abuse. Emotional and mental abuse is often nuanced in a way that is hard to spot because it is more covert than overt. And especially for men, identifying toxicity and abuse in any relationship is challenging as men are programmed, conditioned and groomed to *"Man Up!"* no matter what the circumstance may be. So, men tolerate and accept abuse in relationships, just like women do.

And this is even more prevalent in romantic relationships. However, there are subtle signs of abuse that a man can notice in their partner. A man can get stuck in a toxic & abusive relationship if their partner -

- Has angry or manipulative outbursts
- Purposely withholds sex
- Is overtly flirtatious to get what they want
- Calls the man names in a way that is emasculating
- Says or does things that undermines the man's confidence or puts down their accomplishments
- Interferes with family relationships and causes turmoil
- Accuses them of infidelity
- Embarrasses them in front of family or friends

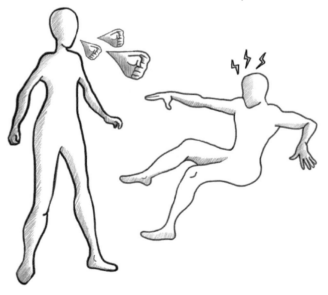

How men experience toxic relationships

Women are more inclined to 'tend and befriend' because women are socialized to reach out and help other people. Men on the other hand, have had a different experience. They have been raised very differently. They have been told to be the strong one, especially in relationships. To push down their feelings. This has only left them in many ways emotionally handicapped.

Men fear sharing what they are experiencing because they feel no one would take them seriously or that people would look down on them, especially their male friends whom they believe would not be supportive.

Men turn to drinking or using drugs to numb the pain so they 'emotionally check out' to manage the internal distress of the toxic relationship. They become more depressed and anxious. They have limited resources and have no idea where or whom to turn to. Eventually, they start to question themselves and begin to doubt themselves.

They feel ashamed that they are in a toxic relationship. Men become hard on themselves saying things like –

"What is wrong with me?"

"I have to stop letting this situation get to me."

Unfortunately, this just reinforces their feelings of shame, isolation, and loneliness. It's a vicious cycle of self-blame and loathing. However, to examine their relationship and determine what their next steps are, the first step is always awareness and recognizing – and admitting – that it is abusive. Once abused men can do that, they can begin to heal.

Editor's Note

Abuse and domestic violence against men is a reality that is often brushed under the carpet. Yet, numerous men across the globe suffer silently in abusive relationships with no hope for help.

As a society we need to acknowledge that men too can be trapped in abusive relationships and offer our support without any judgment or criticism. We need to rise above stereotypes and provide a safe space for abused men to reach out and seek help.

Abuse should never be tolerated, regardless of someone's sex or gender. And it is high time that we all stand united against abuse, without discriminating against men in abusive relationships.

Infidelity and Cheating in Toxic Romantic Relationships

LINDA GREYMAN

Commitment, loyalty and faithfulness often become elusive when a relationship is poisoned with toxicity. A relationship that lacks genuine love will sooner or later become entangled in infidelity and cheating.

In toxic relationships, infidelity can become a repetitive cycle that may continue even when confronted with the truth. Such is the bane of toxic relationships, where both the abused and the abuser can cheat either to feel important or loved.

Are toxic people more likely to cheat?

People with narcissistic traits often lack commitment due to lower relationship satisfaction. As they struggle with their own insecurities and low self-esteem, cheating with multiple partners outside their primary relationship becomes a means for them to boost their inflated ego and reinforce their own distorted self-image. Being successful with multiple sexual partners or getting romantic/sexual attention from others helps them overcome their internal struggles, at the cost of their primary relationship.

Moreover, as toxic individuals are less caring, less empathic and have insecure attachment styles, it is easier for them to cheat on their primary partner without thinking much about the consequences of their actions.

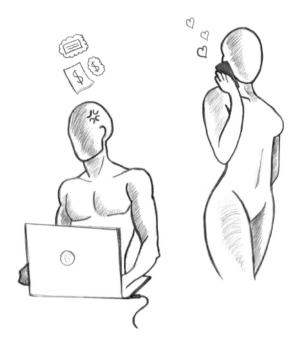

Why does a toxic person cheat?

A toxic person's sexually permissive attitude and tendency to have extramarital affairs is primarily dominated more by the need of having control and power rather than sexual gratification. Regardless, infidelity is a complicated issue that involves subtle nuances which need to be explored.

Here are some factors that can make a toxic person cheat on their spouse or partner –

1. Sexual narcissism

Individuals with narcissistic traits typically have a strong sense of entitlement, and this is applicable even for sexual experiences. Sexual narcissism is driven by a grandiose sense of sexual abilities, sexual entitlement and sexual exploitation.

This can make a narcissist strive to control their own marital and sexual satisfaction.

2. Low self-esteem & insecurities

Toxic people struggle with crippling insecurities and low self-esteem, which makes them desperate for seeking out attention and validation from others as attention from their primary partner simply isn't good enough for them. Moreover, as they feel insecure in the relationship, they choose to cheat on their partner, because to them it is better to reject their primary partner than getting rejected by them.

3. Self-gratification

As toxic people have lower commitment to their relationship and feel less attached to their partner, they are more focused on their self-gratification. They are more concerned about enjoying the moment than the consequences and concerns that come with their actions. To them, an important relationship holds less value than gaining temporary emotional or sexual gratification.

4. Power and Control

Toxic people like to dominate, control and manipulate others in every aspect of life, including sex. This can be especially evident in "enabler" relationships, where the abused partner or the victim accepts toxic behaviors from the abuser. As the toxic person is handed over power over the relationship, they have no fear of any real consequences or repercussions from their partner. So, they boldly engage in serial infidelity.

5. Genetics

The tendency to cheat (or be cheated upon) can be heritable and run in families across generations. Individuals with narcissistic traits are more permissive towards sexual infidelity if they have seen their parents engage in marital infidelity themselves. Awareness of parental sexuality can lead to intergenerational transmission of infidelity and challenges in romantic relationships.

Can victims be cheaters too?

Yes, victims can cheat too but for completely different reasons and motivations. When someone is stuck in a miserable relationship with no hope for recovery, cheating will eventually crop up as an alternative, yet unethical solution to feel "normal", especially when leaving the relationship is difficult.

The non-toxic person can resort to infidelity as a last attempt to boost their self-esteem after being constantly devalued by their toxic partner, especially when they have acted as the "giver" or "enabler" for too long without getting anything in return, except disrespect. This can be especially true when the toxic partner is extremely controlling, possessive & jealous.

Although these should not be considered as a justification for the victim engaging in infidelity, toxic partner's behaviors can often drive the victim to seek attention, admiration, love, respect, value and sexual satisfaction outside the primary relationship.

Affairs are not just about sex

Regardless of who cheats in the relationship, the abuser or the victim, infidelity is more about coping with our internal needs and issues, than enjoyment. This is the reason why it has been reported that individuals with a lack of connection with primary partners experienced a greater intellectual and emotional intimacy in the affair.

Substance Use Disorders and Toxic Relationships

DR. PEG O'CONNOR

Substance Use Disorders (SUDs) and toxic relationships can be intricately connected. They may mutually influence each other, often to very bad effect.

Recovering from a Substance Use Disorder may prompt a person to leave a toxic relationship. Leaving a toxic relationship may open the space for a person to begin to change his, her, or their patterns of consumption.

A toxic concoction

Studies show that there is a strong correlation between Intimate Partner Violence (IPV), which is arguably the most toxic form of a relationship, and Substance Use Disorders. People who are abused are more likely to develop a Substance Use Disorder, perhaps because consuming substances becomes a method to cope or to lessen stress, anxiety, fear, and trauma. Abusers may also compel their victim to drink or use along with them. The one who is abused often becomes highly attuned to the drinking and using patterns of the abuser, especially when that use causes violence.

People who are struggling with a Substance Use Disorder may be especially vulnerable to toxic relationships. At their most severe, substance use disorders can greatly affect cognitive abilities and emotional regulation during active use and beyond. People in this condition may make impulsive choices far removed from their best interests.

They may also believe they do not deserve anything better than toxic or abusive behaviors they experience from others. People with a severe substance use disorder may become resigned to their circumstances, adopting a fatalistic tone that there is absolutely nothing they can do that will make a difference.

Is 'change' possible?

In toxic relationships where both partners have a substance use disorder, one partner deciding to change behaviors may find little support from the other. Moreover, there may be some antagonism and hostility about changing; sabotage may become the new means to control.

The choice to change using patterns may be perceived as an act of disloyalty or even a kind of intimate treason. This may increase the risk of additional and even new forms of toxic and abusive behavior.

Life is worth living

Toxic relationships and substance use disorders separately and combined damage self-trust and trust in others. We often fail to take our own needs, wants, and hopes seriously while giving too much concern to others'.

We and our beliefs don't matter; life may not matter. At the darkest hours, we may believe that our life is not worth living. Psychologist William James (1842-1910), suggests that even the slightest glimmer of belief that it is worth living will help to bring about the fact that it is worth living.

Editor's Note

Overcoming addiction

If you are stuck in a toxic relationship and struggling with substance use, then here are a few ways to start overcoming your addiction –

1. Keep your mind engaged in building healthy, drug-free habits. Cultivate interests that bring you joy, meaning & purpose and learn new skills to shift your focus away from substance use.

2. Set and pursue small goals to show yourself that you can achieve them and change successfully.

3. Practice mindfulness meditation to increase your self-awareness, reduce stress, anxiety and depression, gain better mental & emotional control and find inner peace.

4. Seek help from a medical professional or therapist who can help you identify sources for treatment and support.

5. Seek support from trusted friends, family members and loved ones who are sober and can help you reduce your harmful use or achieve sobriety.

6. Talk about your thoughts, feelings, issues, unmet needs and desires, whether to a loved one, a professional therapist or a local support group.

Supporting Toxic Behavior in Relationships

KIM SAEED

Toxic relationships are a bane that can ruin lives and lead to long-term mental health issues. While it is easy to brand the perpetrator as the "toxic person" or "abuser", we rarely take a look at how we, the victims, promote toxic behaviors in the relationship. In fact, friends and family members can also play a crucial role in supporting the toxic person to engage in abusive behavior.

A toxic relationship falls in the abyss of abuse owing to power imbalances in the relationship. While the toxic person may provoke the non-toxic person to react negatively, the victim struggles with self-control and engages in unhealthy behaviors instead of seeking ways to leave the relationship.

Whether you are the abuser or the abused, it will always be hard to look at your own contributions and take responsibility for your actions. However, being accountable is the only way forward to healing and making empowering decisions for your future.

How the victim supports toxic behavior

All relationships are complex and filled with drama. In healthy relationships, both people put in the effort to resolve issues by making sacrifices and compromises equally. But in toxic relationships both parties drain energy from one another.

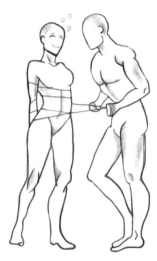

But how can the victim be a part of the problem when they are the one being abused? Here's how -

- They normalize abuse
- They accept all criticisms and accusations from the abuser
- They fail to establish or maintain strict boundaries
- They don't believe in themselves but you believe the lies of the abuser
- They defend the abuser when their friends and family try to support them
- They believe that someday the abuser will change their behavior
- They accept the role of a victim
- They prefer being codependent, not independent
- They exhibit attention-seeking and people pleasing behavior in their relationship
- They react emotionally and not practically

- They deny that they are in an abusive relationship and act needy
- They keep themselves trapped in the cycle of abuse

Accepting how their own behavior may be causing or contributing to the abuse and toxicity can be difficult. But being accountable can enable them to become more aware and overcome toxic patterns.

How friends and family promote toxicity

Toxic people do not operate alone. They have an army of followers who continue the abuse on their behalf to make them appear innocent, while the victim is constantly broken to make them more compliant. This army of supporters acts as flying monkeys to protect and safeguard the abuser.

Toxic people have high expectations from others and will shun or "cancel" them if they don't meet their expectations. So, to avoid being ignored, neglected or abandoned, everyone conforms to the demands of the toxic person. These "flying monkeys" are also captivated by the toxic person's charm and believe that they can do no wrong. As they are unaware of the toxic person's manipulation, they believe the toxic person is the victim and hence, they should be protected. Moreover, these flying monkeys may have their own issues with codependency or low self-esteem, which make them vulnerable to the narcissist's manipulation.

Empathy and toxicity

Empathy plays a crucial role in toxic relationships as most victims tend to be empaths. This is perhaps one of the reasons why they feel so drawn towards toxic individuals as they believe they can help them "change." However, the consequences of unbridled empathy and kindness can be far-reaching.

When people falsely believe that they are responsible for another's offenses or that they can relieve their "suffering," altruism and empathy are misdirected. For instance, a devoted partner believes their weight gain or shorter hairstyle is the cause of their partner's infidelity, or that by changing their hair color, style, or agreeing to outrageous activities in the bedroom, their partner will "never have to cheat anymore."

In the end, manipulative people, such as narcissists, exploit these altruistic inclinations for their own benefit. It is well known that narcissists manipulate empathic and generous individuals. Therefore, it would be best if you took a moment to consider the long-term consequences of your decisions when facing the dilemma of wanting to appear empathetic or when every fiber of your being desires to help someone for whom you feel empathy. Do not make compulsive, potentially devastating decisions that may contribute to the self-centered agendas of the narcissist in your life.

Healthy relationships are possible

Understanding how you or others contribute to the toxic relationship can help you realize how a toxic dynamic plays out. Being aware can better enable you to manage your emotions, properly channel your empathy and take the necessary steps to eradicate toxicity and build a healthier relationship.

Be accountable for your actions, refuse to give in to manipulations and believe that you deserve happiness.

CHAPTER TWO

THE MERCILESS PREDATOR

UNDERSTANDING TOXIC PEOPLE

The Psychology / Mindset of Toxic People

LINDA GREYMAN

Most of us have encountered a toxic person and have some idea about what type of a person they typically are. But what makes them behave the way they do? What drives them to manipulate and abuse others? The better we understand the psychology of a toxic person, the better we will be able to protect ourselves and help them heal.

They are not what they appear

People with toxic traits tend to have a tendency to seek attention, admiration, and affection. This could be because they struggle to deal with their own insecurities and past traumas. In an attempt to cope with these feelings, they may try to control and dominate others. While this can make them appear strong, demanding, and aggressive, in reality they may be desperate for love, empathy, compassion and kindness.

They often prioritize gaining attention, praise, and admiration from others, which can influence their thoughts, actions, and personality. Their focus is often on boosting their self-esteem and concealing their vulnerabilities, which may be an ongoing challenge for them.

Masking their inner weakness

People who exhibit toxic behaviors struggle with feelings of self-hatred and their arrogance may serve as a coping mechanism to mask their vulnerabilities. They may project their distress, misery, and pain onto others as they are unable to confront their own insecurities, shortcomings, and mistakes, which can be emotionally devastating for them.

However, it's important to note that they don't intentionally behave this way. Many of them grow up in dysfunctional families with toxic or abusive parents, leading to the development of insecure attachment styles and the familiarity of toxic behavior patterns from a young age. Alternatively, they may have had overprotective parents who excessively pamper and praise them, which can lead to the development of narcissistic traits.

Behind their facade of confidence and aggression, toxic people may suffer from a lack of genuine connection and purpose. Unfortunately, they may be unaware of their own toxic tendencies and how they affect others. However, they may be aware of their own ability to manipulate, control, and deceive others for their own personal gain.

How toxic people think

Toxic people may have a distorted thought process and an inner voice that prioritizes attention-seeking and boosting their ego. They may tell themselves that they are superior to others and that those who cannot recognize their greatness are somehow deficient.

Their inner voice typically includes thoughts like –

"I am the best. I deserve only the best. Everyone owes me the best of everything."

"Why are they not paying attention to me? Why are they not praising me? Don't they realize how amazing I am? Can't they see I am getting upset? They must be blind idiots."

"How dare they misbehave with me? I will break them and teach them a lesson of a lifetime."

"I can't allow them to spend time with others else they might get

influenced. I need to be stricter and control them even more."

"Only what I want is important. Nothing else matters. And they need to realize that."

"They are so gullible and 'soft'. I can use their 'weaknesses to my own advantage. They won't even see it coming. All I need to do is tell them how much I love them."

These inner voices may be a combination of deep-seated insecurities and a falsely inflated sense of self. This duality can make it challenging to engage with toxic individuals effectively.

Toxic people are complex individuals

Toxic people can be complex individuals, and understanding their mindset and behavior patterns is crucial to managing interactions with them. Those with personality disorders such as narcissism or borderline personality disorder may present unique challenges in this regard. These individuals may struggle to understand their own thoughts, emotions, and inner selves due to deep-seated insecurities and a need to protect their fragile self-image.

It's essential to recognize that some toxic individuals may be aware of their behavior patterns and motivations, but choose to hide or suppress this awareness to avoid confronting uncomfortable truths about themselves. Nevertheless, gaining insight into the psychology of toxic individuals can provide us with effective strategies for engaging with them in a productive and healthy way.

Body Language of Toxic People

LINDA GREYMAN

Toxic people are masters of deception. They can pretend to be highly charismatic and pleasing to hook their victims. And once they have trapped their potential prey, they slowly reveal their real abusive self. However, there is a subtle way to spot a toxic individual during a casual encounter - through their shady body language.

Body language signs of toxicity

Passive aggressive behavior, condescension, and a tendency to avoid eye contact are all subtle signs of toxic behavior that can be indicative of a person's true personality and intentions. Paying attention to these subtle cues can help you identify early warning signs of potential toxic relationships and future heartbreak.

Consider the following body language signs that may help you identify a toxic individual during your initial interactions:

1. Avoiding eye contact

Avoiding eye contact is a telltale sign of dishonesty, nervousness, low confidence, and poor self-esteem. A toxic person will often avoid locking eyes as they are afraid that their lies will be caught. Eye contact makes them feel uncomfortable as they are crippled by their own insecurities and inner conflicts.

Conversely, they may make forced and intentional eye contact so that you don't suspect them of dishonesty. Nevertheless, this will still feel unnatural and uncomfortable, creating a sense of unease for the non-toxic person.

2. Invading personal space

Toxic people often use intimidation tactics to dominate and control others. By invading your personal space, they can make you feel uncomfortable, confined, and submissive. By getting physically close during interactions, they can establish a position of power and manipulate the situation to their advantage.

3. Eye-rolling

They may roll their eyes upwards or sideways when you say something they don't agree with. This behavior can be used to establish their perceived intellectual superiority and make you feel inferior. By rolling their eyes, they may seek to frustrate you, diminish your confidence, and create doubt in your mind without even saying a word.

4. Crossed arms

Toxic individuals often cross their arms as a way to create a sense of separation and defensiveness, particularly when they feel offended. This defensive body language can also indicate discomfort with the conversation or the other person's viewpoint. When a toxic person crosses or clasps their hands in front of them, it can create a physical barrier and convey that they are unapproachable, closed off, and unwilling to consider different perspectives

5. Excessive finger pointing

Finger pointing is a nonverbal way of blaming or accusing someone. This is why toxic people often use it strategically to make others feel vulnerable, defensive and reactive. During interactions, they may constantly point fingers at you, making you feel uncomfortable and defensive. This behavior can feel like a verbal attack, causing distress to your heart and soul. Finger-pointing also allows toxic individuals to sound more assertive and assert dominance in the conversation.

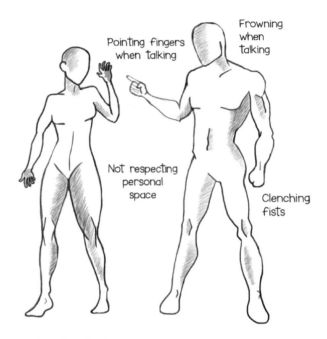

Negative body language cues

Toxic individuals use various other negative body language cues that can reveal their inner toxicity, consciously or subconsciously like:

1. Staring for too long and too intensely to make the other person feel judged, worried and vulnerable.
2. Constantly checking their phone which shows they are disinterested, indifferent, bored and impatient with the person they are interacting with.
3. Frowning a lot while communicating which reveals that they are annoyed, irritated, unhappy and angry yet trying

not to express themselves honestly.

4. Standing with hands behind the back can signify that the toxic person is trying to hide something, being secretive, and cannot be trusted.

5. Clenching their fists which show that the toxic person is aggressive and ready to burst out and get into a fight if provoked.

6. Looking around while talking to someone indicates disrespect and boredom with the current conversation.

7. Not responding to the other person while conversing is a classic sign of toxicity as it shows that the abusive person is not paying attention, agreeing with or listening to the other individual or the victim.

8. Refusing to smile during conversations to show indifference or a lack of emotional involvement in the other person.

9. A jutting chin or lifting the chin forward is a sign of being judgmental, superiority, dominance, aggression, defiance, mockery and challenge.

Toxic behaviors that are easily missed

Identifying toxic or abusive individuals can be challenging, as they may not always exhibit overt signs of their behavior. However, there are some subtle non-verbal cues that can help you recognize potentially toxic individuals during your initial interactions -

1. A sense of superiority

Toxic people believe they are superior to others and often display this through their body language. They may act friendly at first, but will maintain their personal space and behave condescendingly towards others. They may avoid close physical proximity, even though they may willingly invade others' personal space.

2. Seeking special treatment

Toxic people typically have a strong sense of entitlement which makes them believe they are special and deserve VIP treatment everywhere they go. While they may not be overly aggressive, they will be assertive about –

- Demanding faster service
- Not having enough time to wait in queues
- Demanding personalized services
- Monopolizing conversations
- Interacting only with authority figures
- Demanding undivided attention from their partners

As they think that the world revolves around them, they may react aggressively such as storming out of a restaurant or insulting service providers, when denied special treatment.

3. Being extremely charming

Toxic relationships follow a three-stage pattern: idealizing, devaluing, and discarding. During the idealizing phase, toxic people use love-bombing to create a sense of dependency and admiration in their target. They will act charismatic and shower excessive affection and attention on their target to make them feel special, but their true goal is to create dependency.

4. Showing off

Toxic people are prone to bragging about their intellect, abilities, appearance and accomplishments. They constantly claim to have –

- Helped others
- Saved someone's life
- Be highly successful in their career
- Be pursued by many potential suitors

- Be extremely wise, knowledgeable and intelligent

They will confidently pass off others accomplishments and experiences as their own without hesitation. They are nothing but a PARASITE pretending to be a GOD.

5. Impatient and easily bored

Toxic people show no interest in conversation unless it revolves around them. They speak about themselves in a robotic tone, and every conversation is about their greatness. If the topic shifts away from them, they lose interest and won't respond unless it's brought back to them. They don't like being questioned or criticized and may cut off those who doubt them or make fun of their claims.

Body language matters

We often become involved with abusive, toxic people before we can recognize who they truly are. And by the time we see their real toxic self, we are already trapped in their web of abuse and manipulation. We regret being fools for not being able to identify their reality earlier.

However, by being attentive to a person's non-verbal cues and behavior, we can gain valuable insight into their character and protect ourselves from years of harm. So, the next time you meet someone new, take the time to observe and interpret their non-verbal communication. It could save you from a lot of pain in the long run.

Toxic Parents

JULIE L. HALL

People don't like to admit that parents can be abusive toward their children. We prefer to believe that all parents love their kids and have their best interests at heart. The reality, of course, is that dysregulated, selfish, delusional, and even sadistic people have children too. The state of parenthood doesn't magically transform them into human beings capable of the maturity and empathy needed to love children, even their own.

Parents with Cluster B personalities often believe they are good parents, even "perfect" ones, and they may go to great lengths to portray themselves that way to others and convince themselves and their kids that they are. The reality about toxic parents, however, is that they have profound personality deficits and delusions that make them traumatizing to their children.

Traits of toxic parents

1. They are extremely self-referential and see relationships in terms of their own needs and perspective.

2. They demand excessive attention and create dramas to get it.

3. They lack emotional empathy and are unable to consistently care about others' feelings and needs.

4. They struggle with repressed shame and anxiety.

5. They are emotionally dysregulated, quick to anger or panic, and prone to mood swings.

6. They are easily threatened by perceived disrespect and react with overt rage or passive aggression.

7. They violate interpersonal boundaries.

8. They deny things they do not wish to acknowledge or deal with.

9. They project their feelings and behavior onto others, especially those they are abusing.

10. They envy other people's happiness and success and will try to either take ownership of it or sabotage it.

11. They view relationships transitionally and expect to get more than they give.

12. They see vulnerability as weakness and avoid intimacy.

13. They have superficial relationships and value status over substance

14. They are rigid, controlling, and intolerant of differences in others.

15. They see things in binary, all-or-nothing terms.

16. They insist on agreement and compliance with their views and values.

17. They have delusions of being superior to others and entitled to special privileges.

18. They blame, hurt, and humiliate others to feel better about themselves.

19. They refuse accountability in their relationships.

20. They manipulate others through bullying, guilt, and pity-plays.

As a child dealing with the daily volatility and selfishness of your toxic parents, you were subjected to normalized distortions of reality and violations of trust by the people you relied on for your survival. This environment elicited a hypervigilant nervous system (flight/fight) response in you that may have felt like ongoing watchfulness, dread, and anxiety. Because of the relationally unsafe reality you experienced at home and the lack of support for your developmental needs, you probably struggle with internalized shame, low self-esteem, and unclear boundaries. You may also have coping patterns, such as perfectionism or people pleasing, that helped you survive as a child but have become self-defeating in adulthood.

The good news is that as someone working on education and self-awareness, you have already overcome many of the obstacles to recovery that keep your parents trapped in dysfunctional patterns.

Toxic Family / Siblings / Relatives and Friends

CHRISTY PIPER

When you grow up in a toxic family, your siblings will typically be toxic as well. This is because toxicity is learned from other family members, and passed down from generation to generation.

The toxic family dynamic

Even though some may be full blown narcissists and others may just display toxic habits, they still grew up around a negative atmosphere. They may be extremely critical of others. They may smile to your face, then whisper behind your back and laugh about your secrets to others. But if you confront them, they'll act like you are the crazy one. They won't own up to their bad behavior.

There is often crying, drama, and someone being left out. Each person is treated differently. There is a "favorite." Sometimes the position of the "favorite" changes just to keep people confused and on their toes. But usually those who are treated the worst are consistent.

You may have to watch what you say. Even if you do express your feelings, you may feel shut down. You begin to learn your opinions aren't important. Whatever the matriarch or patriarch says, goes.

If you have goals or dreams or accomplish something amazing, your family is likely critical or jealous. Especially if you aren't the favorite. You wonder why they can't be supportive like other families. This lack of support from your tribe can be debilitating even if you don't realize it. It affects your confidence levels and all your social interactions in the world. Not just the ones with your family.

The toxic family hierarchy: Negativity, lack, division, & competition

Your family may criticize you if you say something "negative". They may say you are a mean or bad person, even if they say awful things about others all the time. Much of what you say is taken out of context. It's very frustrating and it feels like no one understands you. If this happens to you, it's because you aren't a favorite in the family hierarchy.

The matriarch or patriarch in the family who everyone looks up to, fears, and worships is the head toxic person. The family dynamics are all about them and their ego. The head is always playing people off each other. Their goal is to keep everyone separated, competitive, and pitted against each other. This is how they keep their power and control. This way they have everyone vying to get their approval. Plus, it keeps others divided so they don't team up against the head toxic person.

To the head matriarch or patriarch, "dividing and conquering" is their strategy. They operate from a place of lack and competition. Petty and unnecessary fighting among relatives is also common in toxic families. The matriarch or patriarch stirs up drama between them, keeping them separated. But most of the family doesn't see it for what it is. To them, it's how life has always been. They don't question the real reasons they fight, or if it's even normal.

Family secrets, speaking up, & shame

From the outside looking in, some people assume your family is normal. Especially if you grew up middle class and dressed well. People may even think you were privileged and lucky. These family secrets kill your spirit, because no one even suspects anything is wrong.

You're either told to not tell anyone else, or it's implied. You are chastised for speaking up for yourself to your family. They may even punish you for this. This leads to you suppressing your needs, and thinking others' needs are more important. These secrets cause a lot of shame and inner turmoil.

Since you're not sure what normal is, it's hard to describe even if someone asks. If you try to bring this toxic dynamic to most of your other relatives, they probably won't know what you're talking about. They may even get mad and tell the other family members what you said. If this happens, expect to be ganged up on. They will make you sorry if you question or speak against them.

When you try to change your behavior or leave, your relatives will try to pull you back in. They will guilt you for trying to leave. They may say things like:

"Blood runs thicker than mud."

"You only get one family."

"Family is more important than anything in life.

"It's hard to be alone."

"No one cares more about you than us"

Outsiders don't understand what you have to contend with. Society will think something is wrong with you if you avoid your family, and may even call you ungrateful. Those from a healthy family can't understand why you'd want to break free. When no one else understands what you are going through, chances are you will keep going back for more pain and insults.

The relationship with your siblings & tension

There was a lot of tension between your siblings growing up. Maybe you still don't get along. Competition and insulting each other were taught and encouraged. Calm times in your household were short lived. Someone always caused drama. There was always something to be upset about. You felt bad and unworthy a lot of the time. But you didn't realize why.

There's a good chance your siblings were pitted against each other. You may have fought a lot, disrespected each other, or just didn't get along. Someone was the favorite, while the others were treated worse. This unfair treatment and favoritism cause a lot of animosity between siblings. This fits the "divide and conquer" strategy. This is how a toxic parent maintains control.

Some toxic parents will still try to keep the siblings separated and against each other as adults.

How your family role affects your friendships?

If you're from a toxic family, they've placed you in a role. And you play this role out in every other relationship in your life to some degree. You are most likely drawn to friend groups with toxic dynamics. The way they speak feels comfortable to you, like home. Even if you don't realize why.

When in a toxic friend group, they make you feel bad most of the time. They put down and criticize others around them, including you. But you likely put up with it because you're used to it. After all, your own family treats each other this way.

There is even a similar hierarchy within this friend group. The head toxic person calls the shots and divides people within the friend group. Inevitably, something about a "friend" will upset the head. They will turn on this "friend," launching a campaign against them. The head will play with this person and torture them, then oust them from the group. This is shameful because it's public humiliation. This friend is now isolated from the group, while the other friends likely won't even speak to them anymore. Eventually most of the friend group will end up despising each other.

You may get into toxic individual friendships. You may find a friend who seems nice at first. But you miss the red flags. Over time, they start to use and abuse you. Until you say no for good, they will drain you of money, favors, or emotional energy.

How feeling excluded from & mistreated in groups affects yourself worth

Over and over, you're made to feel like the black sheep in the group. But it's because of the toxic people you surround yourself with. Healthy people don't treat others this way. You don't know any better, so you internalize it. You may think that you are inherently flawed—that you deserve to be treated badly.

For a lot of your life, you may not realize what is happening. You may feel sad or have a lot of negative feelings. You may think you have mental health issues, or feel like something is wrong with you. This may cause symptoms of depression, social anxiety, or ADHD.

This label becomes part of your identity. But you don't know the root cause. You think it's you, or that it runs in your family. In other words, it seems like there is not much you can do about it. This leads to helpless thinking, instead of empowering yourself to solve the issues.

While depression or anxiety medication can help, it won't fix the root cause - all the toxic friends and family in your life who are bringing you down.

Toxic Partners / Spouse

CHRISTY PIPER

A toxic partner or spouse didn't start out acting like a jerk. They probably seemed like your "dream come true" at first. So, you fell for them hard.

They probably rushed you into moving in, getting married, or having kids together. They moved fast. You probably didn't have much time to think about what was happening or get to know them. They depended on your emotions sweeping you away, and acted like the same thing happened to them. You reasoned that it moved quickly because it was meant to be. Maybe the clincher was when they called you their soul mate, twin flame, or said they knew you were "The One."

Your partner mirrored all your hopes, dreams, interests, and favorite things back to you. So, they felt like your perfect match.

The switch & why it's hard to see it

They made you feel really special. At first. But once they knew their claws were in you, they "changed" and started revealing their true personality. They stopped trying to hide their true self after moving in together, getting married, or having kids.

At some point, you realize you were tricked. The person they showed you at first is not the one you see in front of you. It was an act to get you hooked. Now that you're hooked, they can drop the act. They think you won't leave.

They get you dependent on them early. They try to get you

legally entangled with them as soon as possible. Examples include having a kid together, signing legal (marriage or business) contracts, getting you to quit your job, or putting all your money in a joint bank account with them. They may even convince you to put your property or resources in their name. This makes it more complicated to leave them.

This sounds illogical to an outsider. People wonder how they can get away with this. But it's because they do it very gradually. Sending out little pings to test your boundaries. This is how they figure out what they can get away with. If you try to complain, they will just try another way, or guilt trip or harass you into complying.

Once you're attached to them, they start insulting you and blaming you for anything and everything. You get stuck defending your honor and trying to prove yourself to them. When they switch your focus to your own flaws, they are distracting you from seeing their flaws.

Why they hide their true selves in the beginning

They are masters of playing mind games. They understand what is desirable in a partner, and act accordingly. Since they study you very carefully, they know how to attract you. They make you feel like they are your perfect match and dream partner. You are so excited about this; you want to believe it. So, you buy into it fully.

After this point, they know they have you hooked. No one can tell you anything different, even if all the evidence points to them being toxic and manipulative. People always use their emotions as a basis on which to form logic. So, emotions always trump logic-- no matter what they tell you. A toxic person knows this.

A toxic partner comes from a place of lack

A healthy partner builds up their partner, knowing their partner's happiness will make them happy. But a toxic partner doesn't believe this. They suffer from low self-esteem. They think the only way they can keep a partner around is to trap them.

This includes destroying your self-worth. They do this through constant verbal abuse. If you feel bad about yourself, you probably won't leave. Maybe they tell you how unattractive you are, and that no one else would want you. They may also say you can't survive without them. They'll be sure to remind you of the financial support they provide you, or anything else they do for you.

Another strategy is to limit your money. Whether they convince you to not work, spend all your money, or control your money, it makes it very hard for you to leave when you don't have the resources to do it.

They isolate you to influence you better

A toxic partner doesn't want you to have anyone close to you. They may even move you far away from anyone you know or love. If they isolate you, you depend more on them. And you don't have anyone to lean on or run to if they mistreat you.

They also want to be the only voice in your ear. If you do maintain close friends or family, they will likely be jealous of these people. They don't want anyone else to contradict what they tell you. A toxic partner knows that if no one goes against their viewpoints, you'll eventually believe them-- no matter how wildly untrue their words seem at first.

Public vs. Private persona

Most people in the community probably think they are great.
They likely treat total strangers and acquaintances like gold.

Public Persona

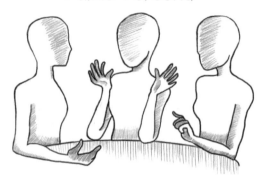

Private Persona

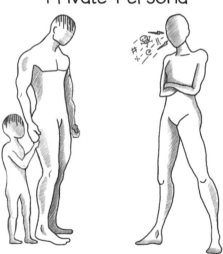

Everyone may love the toxic person in public, including your family and friends. Your partner knows how to put on a good act. They know what to say to get people to like them. Their friends and acquaintances often can't comprehend that your partner is actually abusive.

It's frustrating because no one else sees their toxic behavior. No one can validate your experience. You may feel like you are the problem. You may start to believe that it's your fault you bring out their bad behavior, and that you deserve it.

Desperation & the decision to leave

Despite the bad treatment, you're in denial. You can't believe what you're seeing. You wait for their nice persona to return. The person you first met. When they finally do something nice for you, you feel so happy and relieved. You forget about any plans to leave them. But this is short lived. They go back to mistreating you.

You feel awful. You may cry a lot. You feel guilty and think it's your fault. Your partner who you love blames you for everything. And why would someone who loves you lie to you? This is all done very slowly. So, it may take a long time to figure out something is terribly wrong.

One day you realize you are a shell of yourself. But you have a choice. You can stay or leave. You know it'll be hard to leave. You come up with all the reasons and excuses to stay. Often, it takes the support of caring friends and family to convince you to finally get out. When you do decide to walk away, freedom will be waiting on the other side.

It can take many years to finally leave. It'll take many years after that to finally recover mentally and emotionally.

After effects & recovery

Recovery from all the toxic programming and trauma can take time. You will cry a lot and still feel the emotional ups and downs. It's like getting off a roller coaster, but still feeling like you're on it for a while.

After leaving, you won't feel right. You may interpret this feeling like you can't live without your toxic partner. But if you don't cut off all communication with them, they will likely try to lure you back. Don't give in! It'll be much worse if you go back. Even if they make promises to change. You'll be punished for leaving.

You will start to heal and feel normal eventually. You will need to build your self-esteem and finances back up slowly. This may involve taking a job that you are very overqualified for. But you can work your way up from there into higher positions and pay. Success and positive feedback will help you recover and feel good about yourself again.

It will be hard to trust anyone in a relationship again. When you do start to date again, you can easily get triggered. Small events can remind you of what your toxic partner did to you. Take your time before dating again.

Eventually, you can establish a healthy relationship with someone who truly cares about you. You'll feel safe bringing up these triggers with them, and they can help you heal them.

One day you'll be in a happy relationship if you want it badly enough. Do not sell yourself short.

Toxic Workspace

CHRISTY PIPER

There are toxic people in most workplaces. But they are more likely to be found in certain companies and industries. Workplaces that pay less than the industry standard and have policies that don't value employees are more likely to have more toxic employees. That's because positive people who know their worth don't stay in toxic and disrespectful environments. The ones who stay typically have a negative attitude and complain a lot. Toxic people embody these traits and feed off this unhealthy environment.

Toxic people feel intimidated by those smarter and more educated than themselves. Instead of being happy that they're working with them, the toxic person feels threatened. Toxic coworkers are always on the lookout for an ideal target. This is often someone who is overly nice, or has been abused before. How do they know who to choose? They put out little tests to see how you respond.

They are typically nice at first. But once they peg you as an easy target, it's very hard to get out of this category. They are very prideful and don't like to be wrong. Changing their mind about you would mean admitting they were wrong.

What they look for in a target

They look for someone who they think won't stand up for themselves. It may be someone who doesn't fit in with the rest of your coworkers. As an outsider, this person likely won't have others willing to stick up for them either. They think they can mistreat this person any which way, and they won't say a word. The target won't report them or complain.

If the target does report them, the toxic person will already have an arsenal of write ups against them.

If they see signs that you've been abused before, they will treat you badly, too. In their mind, you share the same secret as them: That you are both used to negative, abusive environments. They don't want positive people to find out. This is why they typically act normal and pleasant around positive people, who wouldn't stand for the toxic person's bad behavior.

How a toxic boss thinks & behaves

Toxic bosses are always looking to make an example out of someone. They rule with fear. They believe this is the best way to maintain their position of power. If someone does not obey them or makes them feel or look bad, they probably become the next target.

A toxic boss gives reactions disproportional to the norm. They will remember any perceived slight forever. It is best to think of them as a sensitive young child. They do underhanded things like overload you with work with not enough time to complete tasks or will give you an unfair schedule.

They may make passive aggressive remarks and make fun of you with other employees behind your back. If coworkers start treating you differently, this could be why. A toxic boss will also pit people against you to try to get you to snap in front of everyone. If you do snap, this will make you look like the crazy one. This discredits you, and works in their favor.

How the toxic person treats their superiors at work

The toxic person in the office controls those below them with fear. But they often act like their superiors' lap dog. They cater to and agree with everything their boss says. Even if their boss is wrong, they agree with them to make their boss feel good. They would not disagree with their boss, because they don't want their boss to have negative feelings towards them.

They know the importance of their boss appreciating them. They know that even in the workplace, emotions trump logic. They build up a feeling of loyalty in their boss. Their boss enjoys having them around. This is because the toxic person is their echo chamber, making them feel good about their decisions.

If anything happens to the toxic person, their boss's favor is their insurance policy. They know their boss has their back.

Their blind followers

They also test out people to see who will follow their orders blindly. They will give potential blind followers tasks that make no sense, to see how they react. If they complain or question them, they likely become the target. But if they obey unquestioningly, they become the toxic persons' favorite.

They use this person for many purposes. They like to reward this person publicly. Especially to show how amazing the blind follower is compared to the target. They love making the target feel bad. They also use the blind follower as a spy. They test the blind follower's true loyalty to see what they report back about the target and others.

The problem is, once someone becomes the toxic person's

blind follower, they are stuck. If they deviate or do anything to get out of this role, they will likely become the new hated target.

The target who'll take the fall

Everything they do is setting the target up to fail. Behind the target's back, they consistently talk badly about them to the big boss.

Why? Because if the toxic person screws up, they have someone to blame. Or if the target does decide to complain against them, the boss won't believe it. In the boss's mind, the target is a seriously incompetent person who is one mistake away from getting fired.

By the time either scenario happens, the toxic person has poisoned their boss with all the little things the target does wrong. The big boss won't hear or believe it when the target tells their true story.

Tactics, results & aftermath

A toxic person purposely keeps people on edge and makes them feel watched and fearful. A toxic coworker's intimidation tactics are designed to make the target feel awful. This leads to stress, anxiety, depression, even thoughts of suicide. Many times, the target feels hopeless. As if they are stuck in their situation and completely alone.

Needless to say, a target's performance will likely suffer. Their mind is constantly on edge, due to this abuse. This will give the toxic boss the ammunition they need to write the target up, make them look bad, and get rid of them.

No one else truly knows what the target goes through. None of the coworkers see the full picture of how the toxic person treats the target privately. Because the target is treated so disrespectfully, coworkers may think the target did something to deserve it. By this point, they have probably also been conditioned by the toxic person to dislike the target.

The toxic coworker often finds allies to help write up statements against the target, too. This way they have others to back them up. The target may not realize this is actually bullying. A toxic person can cause the target to question their self-worth, abilities, and value as an employee.

The effects of this can last for years—even after the target leaves the situation. It's best if the target can talk to a professional about what happened. This will help them regain their self-esteem and heal. The right professional can also teach someone how to spot and handle a toxic work situation quickly and effectively next time.

The Initial Charm of Toxic People

LINDA GREYMAN

Toxic people seem to have God-level charisma and charm that can woo even the coldest heart. Even though they are entitled and selfish individuals who can suck the life out of their victims, they never fail to impress and capture the attention of those they prey upon.

But why are toxic people so charismatic? How do they use their charisma to trap their victims? It is a manipulative psychological game at which toxic individuals excel, employing cunning tactics to achieve their aims.

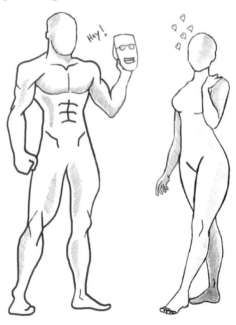

How toxic people charm their prey

You see them staring deep into your eyes, gazing into your soul. You feel goose bumps all over you as your eyes meet theirs. Their soft smile makes you feel drawn towards them as if they feel like home. They seem interested in everything about you and intently listen to every single word you say. They laugh at your silly jokes, they understand your struggles, they agree to your opinion, and they share your values. They praise you for being so strong. They notice and compliment even the smallest things about you.

They validate your feelings, they respect your thoughts and choices, they appreciate your appearance just as you are and they believe you are the most important person they have ever met. To them, your needs, desires and wishes are top priority. You feel flattered, special, important, safe and loved. You feel genuinely happy after the longest time. You feel valued, heard and admired. You feel like a void is getting filled as you become more and more drawn towards them.

They start spending more and more time with you and you start feeling increasingly flattered. Your insecurities and anxieties take a back seat and you feel you finally found the one who just gets you. This is how the initial charm of a toxic person hooks their prey.

The deceptive tactics of toxic charm

As toxic individuals aren't inherently charming, they use a number of strategies to create the appearance of a natural-born charismatic person. Here are some of the tactics toxic people use to appear pleasing and charming

1.   They create a great first impression.

Being masters of leaving lasting impressions, toxic individuals can create the perfect initial impression with their self-obsession, confidence, appearance, status, humor, eccentricity and sociability.

2. They shower you with praise.

As the compliments flow freely and constantly, their victims can't help but believe their lies as it builds their self-esteem. But it is only a strategy to gain your trust.

3. They pretend to be perfect.

Toxic people can easily make you believe that they are just the person you were looking for. They can easily manipulate you to believe you share a close emotional connection with them and that they are your "soul mate".

4. They pay you a LOT of attention.

Toxic people are aware of the fact that paying undivided attention to someone is the shortcut to getting their attention in return. By giving someone their constant attention, they can easily charm and flatter their victim by making them feel special. But the end goal is to make you dependent on them.

5. They use "mirroring" effectively.

Mirroring is a nonverbal body language strategy where someone imitates the expressions, gestures, mannerisms, attitude and vocal inflections of another while interacting. Toxic people mirror their victims to show they have a similar mindset and attitude.

6. They appear successful by taking credit for the achievements of others.

7. They seem confident and successful due to their ability to gain control and power in professional and social settings (through manipulation obviously).

8. They are excellent storytellers and can captivate audiences by sharing interesting anecdotes, facts, trivia and statistics.

9. They pretend to be broken and tell people they are victims of abuse, either in their childhood or current relationship, to gain their sympathy, empathy, kindness and compassion.

10. They say exactly what the other person wants to hear, even if it is inappropriate. They express their love openly and compel you to commit yourself to the relationship.

From charismatic to manipulative

While you may be enamored by their charismatic personality, soon things take a drastic turn as their sweet, charming personality slowly starts to fade and their reality begins to emerge. The façade of their false initial charm is eventually replaced by avoidance, manipulation and abandonment. Once they have gained your trust, their appearance of being innocent and charismatic is quickly shed, making you wonder who this person is in reality.

You are left confused as they start exhibiting toxic behaviors. They become more demanding, controlling and dominating. Gradually, the toxic person may-

- Seem detached and disconnected
- Seem bored and uninterested in you
- Appear withdrawn and pay little attention to you
- Disagree with you all the time
- Criticize and devalue you
- Make decisions for you
- Seem interested in others more than you

- Focus more on themselves than you

You cannot figure out what exactly happened and start doubting yourself. You blame yourself for not being good enough for the toxic person and for not being able to maintain their interest. Your insecurities and anxieties become magnified as you become desperate to recapture their attention and get them back to their charismatic self. And that is exactly when you step into their trap.

You lower your guards, break your boundaries, compromise your values and accept toxicity and abuse... all because you want them to appreciate you like they used to. But alas, that charming person cannot be found anywhere anymore. However, as the cycle of abuse repeats itself, the toxic person will become charming again, preventing you from leaving them and making you addicted to them once again. This is the game the charismatic abuser plays with their victims.

Fake charm, real toxicity

A toxic person's charm is a weapon to bait their prey and trap them in their web of abuse. While it may initially make you think like you found the person of your dreams, in reality, they are a manifestation of your worst nightmare. The moment you let your guards down and give them your trust, they will instantly suck out all your energy and use you to their advantage.

However, being aware of the red flags and being vigilant can help you identify their toxic charm to protect yourself. Remember, if it feels too good to be true, then it probably is.

Understanding Abuser Personalities

DR. ELINOR GREENBERG

It can be tempting to dismiss all abusers as narcissists. In fact, if you have been spending time on the internet these last few years, you will find that many people seem to assume that all toxic relationships involve someone with a narcissistic personality disorder. Unfortunately, the truth is far more complicated.

There are two things common to all personality disorders that increase the likelihood that someone with any personality disorder might become abusive:

- A lack of whole object relations
- A lack of object constancy

What is a lack of whole object relations?

Whole object relations (WOR) are the psychology term for the capacity to see oneself and other people in a realistic, stable, and integrated way that simultaneously contains both liked and disliked characteristics. If you do not have WOR, you can only split and see people as either all-good or all-bad.

One of the strange things about a lack of WOR is that when you switch to seeing someone as all-bad, you instantly "forget" all the positive interactions you ever had with this person in the past.

What is a lack of object constancy?

Object constancy (OC) is closely related to whole object relations. If you lack object constancy, when you feel hurt, frustrated, disappointed, angry, or even physically distant from someone, you lose touch with all of your positive feelings for that person. You can go from love to hatred in a heartbeat.

A lack of object constancy is one of the main reasons why people abuse the person that they claim to love.

A lack of OC means that when you are in a fight, you are much more likely to abuse your lover because you now see your mate as your enemy.

You know all those news stories where a man batters his wife to death and then is shown crying, saying: *"I love her. I never meant to do this. She was my whole life!"* Well, some of those men are telling the truth.

What happened is that he lacks object constancy. They got into a fight. He split from seeing her as his all-good beloved wife and, in the heat of the moment, she became his hated enemy. That led to him battering her. Once he was no longer angry at her, he split back and now sees that he has killed the person he loves. This same lack of WOR and OC is directly responsible for a lot of child abuse.

While all people with personality disorders lack WOR and OC from an object relations theoretical point of view, each personality disorder has a somewhat different profile about why they split and how they act when they split on someone they claim to love.

What causes people with BPD to abuse their mates?

People with borderline personality disorder (BPD) are extremely sensitive to feeling unloved and abandoned. Because they lack WOR and OC, anything that they experience as abandonment will cause them to split and see their mate as their enemy. Here is an example of how that

115

leads to borderline abuse.

Betty and Carlos' Story

Betty loved Carlos and Carlos loved Betty. However, Betty has BPD and is too low functioning to manage her feelings of abandonment without becoming violently angry. When Carlos told her that he was going out for drinks with the guys after work, she felt furious at him. She became convinced that he was with another woman.

Betty followed him to the bar to check on him. She brought a baseball bat with her. When she saw Carlos's car parked outside the bar, she bashed out all his windows. Then she entered the bar and angrily confronted Carlos. However, he acted loving and pointed out that he was doing exactly what he had said. He was having a drink with the guys. There was no other woman.

Betty and Carlos kissed and made up and went home and had passionate makeup sex. This was what their relationship was like: love, splitting, chaos, violence, and passionate kisses.

What causes people with Schizoid PD to abuse their mate?

The abuse pattern of violently abusive people with SPD is more subtle and is caused by different things. People with SPD feel unsafe with other people, even their partners. They are sensitive to feeling intruded upon, dominated, and trapped. They do not know how to negotiate differences, so they do one or more of the following when they feel unsafe:

- They leave without any explanation.
- They take a lover to dilute the intimacy of their main relationship.
- They go in and out of the relationship. They leave when they feel trapped and when their fear diminishes, they

miss the person and ask to come back. They may repeat this in-and-out pattern as long as their mate allows it.

Most people, who are not familiar with schizoid relationship behavior, assume that when any of the above events occur, they are dealing with a narcissist who is hurting them on purpose. The truth is that while people with NPD often leave, cheat, and want to come back, they do this for different reasons than people with SPD.

What causes people with NPD to abuse their mate?

Narcissists lose WOR and OC when they feel disrespected, and they are hypersensitive to minor slights. They see themselves as the victim and feel justified in attacking. Narcissistic abuse can vary from devaluation to physical violence. Unlike people with BPD or SPD, narcissists lack emotional empathy. This means that they do not automatically feel bad if they hurt their mate. If they are a malignant narcissist, they take a sadistic delight in retaliating for some imagined slight.

Punchline: The best predictor of toxic behavior and abuse is the lack of whole object relations and object constancy, not the diagnosis.

How Toxic Individuals Condition and Groom the Victim?

JULIE L. HALL

It may sound harsh to call narcissists and sociopaths predators, yet the descriptor is accurate. Rather than seeing other people as members of the same human tribe, toxic types view others as competitors whom they seek to dominate, exploit, shame, and in more extreme cases destroy.

Simply put, the way a narcissist treats other people can be compared to how one species prey on another in nature, as, for example, hawks' prey on rabbits. But for narcissistic humans, they see other members of their own species predatorily, and that includes their own partners and family members.

Yet narcissists live in society with the same rules and roles as anyone else. Like the rest of us, they learn about fairness, right and wrong, and what is socially accepted and what isn't, and they have responsibilities, careers, and families. So, for the predatory narcissist it becomes necessary to mask their hostile and opportunistic impulses so they can function in society. The more skilled they are at masking, the more successful they will be at getting what they want from others.

Love-bombing

Toxic people often see other people as foe rather than friends, yet also rely on others to give them the attention and affirmation they need to manage their unstable self-esteem. Hence, narcissists often become quite skilled at conditioning those around them into a state of compliance, if not submission. In new relationships, whether friendships or romances, narcissists usually follow a pattern that begins with intense idealizing attention, or love-bombing. This can include behaviors such as the following:

1. Showering you with compliments and praise
2. Calling and texting you frequently
3. Wanting to spend lots of time together
4. Mirroring your interests and values
5. Rushing to intimacy
6. Eliciting sympathy about former "unstable" or "abusive" friends/partners
7. Making premature declarations of affection
8. Inviting you to travel or move in together
9. Fantasizing about your future together
10. Promising commitment

For those targeted with love-bombing, it can feel intoxicating, especially if you grew up with narcissistic or otherwise emotionally immature or withholding parents. Finally, someone is seeing you and thinks you're amazing. Finally, you are getting the love and attention you've always longed for. For these reasons you lower your boundaries and relinquish your normal caution.

Conditioning others to accept abuse

Narcissists in the love-bombing stage of a relationship are often infatuated and project their own feelings of specialness onto you. They also gather information about your likes and dislikes, your hopes and desires, and your vulnerabilities, and they push you to find out how much you will acquiesce to their control and boundary violations.

As infatuation fades and reality settles in, the narcissist increasingly withdraws affection and replaces it with episodes of criticism, blame, and rage. Gradually you get used to living in a state of hypervigilant doubt and fear. Over time the abuser breaks down your sense of self and independence from the relationship by doing the following:

1. Undermining your self-confidence with denials and belittlement
2. Pathologizing your needs and emotional responses
3. Gaslighting your perceptions of reality
4. Punishing you with stonewalling, silent treatment, and rage outbursts
5. Burdening you with excessive responsibilities and problems
6. Manipulating you with guilt and pity plays
7. Sabotaging your moments of happiness and success
8. Attacking your vulnerability
9. Dismissing your interests, strengths, and accomplishments
10. Isolating you from family and friends

But along with the abuse, the narcissist keeps you coming back for more by interspersing it with affection, praise, and promises. You blame yourself for the problems in the relationship, working harder to avoid conflict and win back the "love" you felt early in the relationship. At this point you are trauma bonded to the narcissist and perhaps physically addicted to the roller coaster of abuse and positive reinforcement you've been subjected to.

Katya's Story

Katya and Darian met online and felt immediate attraction. Katya had grown up with an alcoholic father who frequently lectured, criticized, and raged at her and her mother. She was drawn to Darian's soft-spoken vulnerability and how interested he was in hearing her thoughts and feelings. He talked about his domineering mother and difficulty getting the respect he deserved at work. When he asked her to move into his apartment after only a month, she was surprised but agreed because of how attentive he was and how they seemed to agree about so many things. She knew he lacked confidence, but she thought she could help him with that.

Soon after Katya moved in, Darian lost his job and began relying on her financially. He had big dreams for a writing career, which she supported, but had trouble focusing and got defensive if she asked about it. Sexually, Darian said he wasn't able to be interested unless his particular needs were met, which increasingly included things that made Katya feel uncomfortable, even humiliated. When she expressed her feelings, he was dismissive and sometimes refused to talk for hours or even days. To avoid conflict, she withdrew and spent more time on her computer, as Darian was doing. When he accused her of cheating, she worked harder to prove her love.

One evening when Katya came home from work, her key to the apartment didn't work. Darian had changed the locks and told their friends she had betrayed him with someone else. Later Katya learned that Darian had been the one having an affair, and his new girlfriend had taken her place in his apartment.

Identifying Toxic People

CHRISTINA (COMMON EGO)

Before we dive into the topic of toxic people, let's get one thing straight: When we talk about toxicity, we're really referring to the behaviors people exhibit and not the person as a whole. As you've probably noticed, some people can be a toxic influence to you and possibly even seem like a positive influence to another.

So, your experience with anyone is always going to be subjective. But that doesn't make it less real. Your experience with someone is part of your reality, and as such, you have a right to remove any toxicity from your life as you see fit.

Now, you might be wondering what kind of guidelines you can use to define someone as a toxic influence. So here it is.

Anybody whose actions repeatedly cause you pain is considered a toxic influence.

Signs you're dealing with a toxic influence

There are a few key signs that will help you to identify whether someone is a toxic influence in your life:

1. They make you feel bad about yourself

This could be through put-downs, backhanded compliments, or any kind of manipulative behavior designed to make you question your self-worth.

2. They don't listen to you

Toxic people will often steamroll conversations and won't take the time to really listen to what you have to say. They might also interrupt frequently or talk over you without giving you a chance.

3.   They're never wrong

In the eyes of a toxic person, they can do no wrong. They will always find someone or something else to blame and will never take responsibility for their own actions.

4.   They're excessively manipulative

Toxic people often use manipulation tactics to get what they want from others. This could be anything from emotional blackmail to gaslighting (a form of psychological manipulation that causes you to question your own memories or perceptions).

5.   They suck the life out of you

Spending time with a toxic person can be draining and exhausting. You might feel like you need to "walk on eggshells" around them or tiptoe around their feelings.

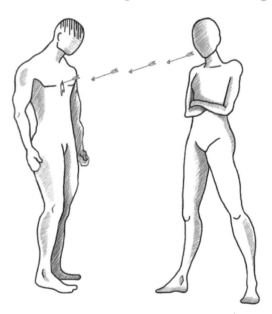

6. You always feel worse after spending time with them

If you find that your mood dips every time you spend time with someone, it's a sign that they might be toxic for you.

Real-life examples of toxic people

Sometimes it can be helpful to see toxic behavior in action to better understand what it looks like. Here are some real-life examples of toxic people and their behavior:

- A boss who is always finding fault with your work, no matter how hard you try.
- A friend who is constantly putting you down, making fun of you, or making snide comments about your appearance or intelligence.
- A family member who belittles and criticizes you at every opportunity.
- A partner who is always trying to control or manipulate you into doing things they want.
- A coworker who is always trying to stir up drama or create conflict.

Toxic influences exhibit behaviors that have a harmful effect on your life. They might be manipulative, aggressive, or paranoid. And if you want to live a more peaceful and fulfilled life, it's important to be able to identify and avoid these toxic influences.

Identifying an Abuser on the First Date

KAYTEE GILLIS

When getting into a new relationship, it is important to be able to recognize red flags. This is especially important if you are trying to avoid starting a new relationship with a potentially toxic person.

People can be misunderstood, especially if they are nervous in a new situation, but look for patterns in how they treat you and others. Getting out of a potentially abusive relationship is easier in the beginning before you become trauma bonded.

There are many ways dysfunctional and potentially abusive patterns can manifest in a budding relationship. And while there is no scientific way to determine if someone is capable of psychological abuse on the first date, these five red flags should be a warning.

Five things to look out for on a first date

1. Bashing their ex-partner/parent of their child

If a new dating partner is speaking disrespectfully or cruelly about others on their first date with you, this is a huge red flag. It shows an enormous lack of respect for others, for you, and ultimately speaks to their integrity.

This is not to say that people are not allowed to have animosity or a bad history with a previous partner. But there is an appropriate way and time to discuss concerns and issues about previous partners, so watch how this is done. Mentioning a concern or issue is different from bashing a

125

person maliciously. Watch for unresolved anger and resentment.

Remember: If they do it to others, they can do it to you.

2. Moving too fast

If they are talking about wanting to be with you forever, wanting to get married, or planning your future together-these should be counted as major red flags.

While there is no standard timeline for sexual intimacy or staying at each other's place, pay attention to when you feel their request seems out of line and they think you can't decline it: This is a violation of your boundaries.

3. Strong sense of entitlement and how they treat other people

Are they rude to the server and valet? Watching how a new date speaks to wait staff is very telling. If they are kind to you but rude to others, this is a red flag that their behavior is not genuine. If they can be cruel to another living thing without feeling remorse, they can- and will- do this to you

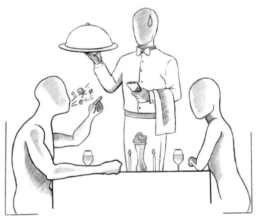

4. Everything is always someone else's fault.

If someone does not take any responsibility or ownership for their behaviors or their part in a disagreement, this should be a huge warning sign that they will not be able to have the self-reflection and self-awareness required for a healthy relationship.

5. Lack of empathy or compassion

The absence of basic human compassion may indicate a lack of guilt or remorse for harming others. While it can be difficult to notice this on the first date, pay attention to how they treat other people, how they talk about others in your presence, and just the overall feeling that you get around them. Do you feel uneasy or uncomfortable?

The opposite is also true: If you feel that they are perfect or too good to be true, they probably are. Pay attention to the amount of time you spend trying to decipher untruths or lies. When you catch yourself saying, *"That just does not make any sense,"* trust that feeling.

Editor's Note

While first dates can be confusing and anxiety-ridden for some people, learning how to spot alarming behavior early on can help you better understand the situation and know what you are getting into with a future partner. Acting smart can help you avoid abuse and heartache down the road. Never settle for less than what you deserve.

Sex and Intimacy
with Toxic Partners

LINDA GREYMAN

Sex and intimacy play a crucial role in any relationship and can be an excellent indicator of whether your relationship is healthy or toxic. Toxic people love playing games in romantic relationships and sex is often another tool for them to boost their ego and to manipulate their partner.

They never hesitate to exploit or take advantage of people who love them, and this is why sex with a toxic partner often feels uncomfortable, even when you give your consent.

Toxic sexual behavior in relationships

When the relationship first started, everything looked too good to be true. Your partner seemed loving, caring, respectful, sensitive, committed and thoughtful. Your sexual experiences were filled with love, tenderness, positive energy and romance. But as time went on, things started to change and you couldn't figure out what was going wrong. It started becoming more about what they want than building a connection.

Your toxic partner started showing signs of superiority and entitlement and demanded affection, praise and sex. While they still respected your consent, they made you feel exploited, used and abused.

Sexual relationship with a toxic partner can make you feel that your partner –

- Only cares about their own sexual pleasure and not about bonding

- Wants you to satisfy their sexual needs and avoid yours
- Seeks praise and compliments about their sexual performance
- Reacts negatively when you refuse sex or specific acts
- Feels entitled to sex and doesn't care about your feelings or mood

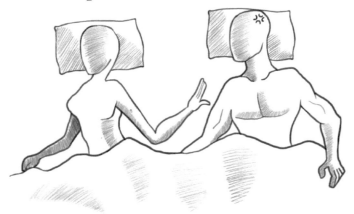

When you refuse sex, they may become angry, manipulative, deceiving, controlling, threatening and even abusive. They may call you unfaithful and often resort to sexual coercion to get what they want.

Sex as a weapon of manipulation

For toxic people, sex is a weapon to bring the other person down to their knees. They want you to think they are the best lover you (or anybody else) ever had. They don't care about making love, being vulnerable or intimate with you. They only care about gaining power and control. So, if you feel used after having sex with a toxic person, it is because they never cared about you. They simply use you as a means to boost their ego. And this is one of the main reasons why toxic people cheat so often in relationships.

Your needs, desires and emotions are unimportant and useless to them. While they may still make you feel loved, wanted, desired and happy at times, it is only to better use you for their own purposes.

The web of sexual coercion

Toxic, manipulative people often use deception, tricks, emotional manipulation and even outright threats to demand sex from unwilling partners by making them feel afraid, guilty or ashamed. This is known as sexual coercion.

They may manipulate their partner to have sex with them by using substances like drugs and alcohol without their consent or against their will. While they may not force you down, they can still use nonviolent manipulative ways to make you comply.

A toxic person can use a wide variety of sexual coercion strategies to control the victim, such as -

1. Deceiving or exploiting their partner for sex, such as saying they are in love with them
2. Threatening them with a breakup, divorce or infidelity
3. Manipulating the victim by accusing them of cheating, being unloving or by showing sadness
4. Creating pressure by begging, whining, nagging and being persistent
5. Intimidating them by devaluing or insulting them and showing aggression
6. Making them feel helpless and hopeless by using the silent treatment or bullying

7. Being physically aggressive during non-sexual arguments making them fear the consequences of saying "no"

Sexual coercion may often sound like –

"If you really love me, then prove it."

"If you don't want to have sex, then I can do it with someone else."

"But I love you so much. Don't break my heart."

"I am so tired of your excuses. If you say 'no' one more time, I'll break up with you"

"You're lucky to have me. No one else would ever touch you."

The degree of sexual coercion can vary depending upon the toxic individual and the relationship. When coercion becomes a repeated pattern, it can become sexual abuse.

Are you being manipulated into having sex?

When it comes to sex, toxic people can use different strategies to sexually use and abuse their partner. When you are in a sexual relationship with a toxic partner, you may experience the following –

1. Your partner makes sudden sexual demands
2. Your partner becomes angry and criticizes when you refuse
3. Your partner uses manipulation or passive aggression to make you comply
4. Your partner pretends to be upset and unloved to gain your sympathy
5. Your partner threatens to cheat on you whenever you refuse sex
6. Your partner is always a taker and never a giver of pleasure
7. Your partner doesn't respect your boundaries in the bedroom

8. Your partner makes you feel unsafe by engaging in high-risk sexual behavior
9. You feel degraded and devalued after having sex
10. You feel sex is more like a duty than a need or desire
11. You feel like being used for sex as it lacks intimacy or connection
12. You blame yourself and feel ashamed for not meeting your partner's sexual needs.

What does it mean if the sex is really good?

For some, sex in toxic relationships can often feel really passionate and exciting, especially after an intense argument or a breakup. Sex can often act as a band aid that hides the toxicity and drama, making you feel great about yourself, your partner and the relationship. Make-up sex feels great because we use it as a coping mechanism to get over all the negativity and heartbreak. However, the toxicity will still exist even after you come out of the bedroom.

Unfortunately, the repeated thrill and excitement of good make-up sex can keep you trapped in a bad, unhealthy relationship longer than you should. And toxic people know how to show you love and passion in restricted doses so that you stay hooked and addicted to them. They will do it in a way so that you feel insecure in the relationship yet submit fully to your partner, in order to get more of the feel-good sexual experience.

Regardless, simply because someone has a "toxic" personality disorder, such as narcissism, does not necessarily mean that they will use manipulation tactics, sexual coercion or cheat on their partner as "toxicity" lies on a spectrum.

CHAPTER THREE

THE UNSUSPECTING PREY

UNDERSTANDING THE VICTIM

The Psychology of the Abused

JESSTON WILLIAMS

Almost all of us at some points have either known of someone or heard of someone who has been the victim of narcissistic abuse. Few of us, however, truly understand the psychology and mindset of such victims.

It can be quite shocking to see someone you know become the victim of narcissistic abuse, as it can be hard to understand how such a person could become so entrenched in the situation. How someone who had always been strong-willed and confident, for example, can gradually become subdued and withdrawn, entering a cycle of victimization that is difficult to break.

It's important to understand that the mindset and psychology of victims of abuse can be complex and varied, as each individual's experience is unique. However, there are some common themes and patterns that are often seen in people who have experienced this type of abuse.

Psychological effects of abuse

Here are some of the common psychological effects of narcissistic abuse:

1. Low self-esteem

Abuse can leave you feeling worthless and undeserving of love and respect. The constant criticism can cause you to doubt your own abilities and value as a person. You may also even begin to blame yourself for the abuse and feel like you deserved it in some way.

2.   Anxiety and depression

Emotional abuse can cause serious anxiety and depression. The constant fear of being criticized or punished can lead to anxiety, while the constant denigration and manipulation can often lead to serious depression.

3.   Trust issues

The constant manipulation and gaslighting can make it difficult to trust your own thoughts and feelings, and you may start to doubt the intentions of others. This can cause you to develop serious questions about your own sanity and lead to withdrawal from friends and family.

4.   Hypervigilance

Due to the unpredictable and often volatile behavior of the abuser, you may feel constantly on guard, always anticipating the next attack or manipulation. This can lead to a heightened state of alertness known as hypervigilance, often caused by some type of trauma.

5.   Fear

Victims of narcissistic abuse may feel afraid of the abuser and their reactions, which can lead to you experiencing feelings of helplessness and isolation.

6.   Fear of abandonment

Toxic people often use the threat of abandonment as a form of control. They may make you feel like you need them and that you can't survive without them. This can lead to a fear of abandonment and a reluctance to leave the abusive relationship.

7.   Feelings of guilt and shame

Narcissistic people may make you feel like the abuse is your fault or that you're responsible for their behavior. This can lead to feelings of guilt and shame, even though you're the one who has been victimized.

8.   Difficulty setting boundaries

The hallmark of narcissistic individuals is that they often have no respect for boundaries. They may constantly invade your personal space or be very demanding. This can make it difficult for you to set and enforce boundaries in your life.

9.   Difficulty trusting your own instincts

Abusers often gaslight their victims, causing you to doubt your own instincts and intuition. This can make it difficult to trust your own judgment and make decisions in your own best interests.

Editor's Note

Inside the mind of the victim

"I am the problem in this relationship. He is not a bad person; I just provoke him to react that way. He loves me, I know it. I don't know what is wrong with me. I need to try harder to make this relationship work."

When you peek inside the mind of an abuse victim, you will see a different story play out in each battered mind. But for most of them, the above narrative is common - *"I am the problem."* Fear, doubt, pain, loneliness, hopelessness, helplessness and a feeling of being unworthy of love darken the light inside their mind.

What was once a strong willed, independent individual has now been reduced to a submissive abuse victim. They feel like being trapped in a dark, desolate forest of toxicity where the abuser is on the prowl to hunt them.

So, they learn to read the atmosphere. They learn to sense the tension in the air. They learn how to anticipate another episode of abuse. They learn to be submissive, to be detached and to diffuse the toxicity.

"If I stay quiet and agree with him, he will calm down sooner."

The more abuse they tolerate, the better they become in reading their abuser. Yet, they still get surprised when the gentle smile on their abuser's face instantly turns sinister. But it teaches them to be more vigilant and be better at sensing the mood in the room. They learn to live with constant anxiety of anticipating the next moment and preparing for the next time their abuser becomes malicious again.

They learn to obey, conform and follow the unspoken rules of the relationship. They modify and transform their thoughts, emotions, words, mindset, attitude and personality to meet the needs of their abuser. Changing the "self" becomes a survival mechanism to protect them from guaranteed harm.

Abuse is not "normal"

Abuse can leave scars that take time, patience and understanding to heal. With that said, the first step to healing from abuse is to recognize that you are in fact being abused in the first place. This can be difficult, as you may already doubt your own judgment due to gaslighting. But if you're constantly feeling criticized, belittled, or manipulated, it's important to acknowledge that it's not normal or acceptable behavior.

Healing from abuse can be a complex and challenging process. It requires a willingness to shift your mindset from being a helpless victim to acknowledging your reality and addressing the psychological and emotional effects of the abuse through consistent self-care and self-compassion.

With time and effort, it's possible to heal and move forward, and to create a life that is full of joy, meaning, and purpose.

Body Language of the Abused / Victim

DR. MARIETTE JANSEN

Have you ever found yourself in a situation where you thought?

"How does this person seem to know so much about me, even though I haven't told them?"

The answer is that you have told them, but not in words. Maybe through your facial expression, your postures, movements, mannerism or the tone of your voice, you have given away information about yourself. And this other person has picked up on it. Sometimes consciously, often subconsciously.

The power of body language

Have you ever felt attracted to someone or wanted to stay away from them? That's because you would have picked up on their body language.

The power of body language as an expression of someone's mindset and intention is often undervalued. Understanding and knowing the body language of victims of emotional abuse will help you to recognize them and approach or support them in the most appropriate way. If you are a victim, paying attention to your body language will help you to 'hide' your experiences from others.

Professor Albert Mehrabian (UCLA) has done research into the impact of non-verbal communications and has come to an oversimplified model, stating that:

- 7% of spoken content is picked up and retained – words only
- 38% of the way the words are spoken is remembered – tone of voice, loudness, roughness
- 55% of non-verbal elements are recollected – the energy field around the person, such as agitation, calmness, confidence or trust.

Reading the abused victims' body language

The left-overs of abuse are fear, low self-esteem, guilt, an external frame of reference and an unhealthy focus on others. What are the body language characteristics that represent these messages?

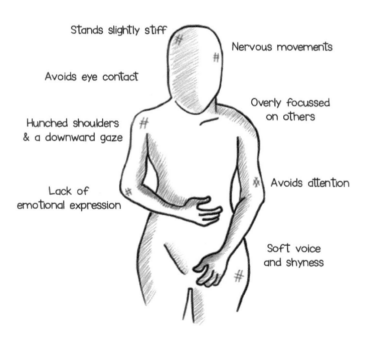

1. Rigidness in the body

They stand slightly stiff; you can tell they are not at ease in their body. They don't move naturally, don't know where to put their hands and ooze a sense of nervousness. They might fidget and show nervous movements, like finger clicking.

2. No eye contacts

They struggle maintaining eye contact. It's too scary as they are more comfortable to hide themselves and eyes reveal the soul, they don't lie

3. Drinking you in

They are overly focused on you to the extent that it makes you feel uncomfortable. It's too intense, too much. Everything you say is great, they nod, laugh even when it isn't really funny, they ask questions about you and won't talk about themselves. They will even physically lean into you.

4. Poor posture

Posture is also a significant indication of the level of confidence: hunched shoulders and a downward gaze usually represent lack of self-esteem. If you compare this to confident people, who stand tall, look around, smile and make eye contact, you will know the difference

5. Lack of emotional expression

Victims can't freely laugh as they can't trust anything or anybody. They will laugh when they think it is the right thing to do, but you can't see the smile in their eyes.

6. Avoiding attention

When asked a direct question or being put on the spot, victims fluster. They don't really know themselves or what they want, as they have been focused on surviving their abuser rather than getting close to themselves. It is also uncomfortable to get attention as attention is connected with danger. It feels safer to hide and not be seen. They prefer to stay in the background.

General shyness can also manifest itself in a soft voice and tentative speaking.

Handle with care

Body language is a great indicator of what might be going on for someone. It is best to use it as a starting point to check out and not use it to form conclusions. A combination of signals combined with a dialogue and observing behavior might confirm or contradict the suspicion that someone is an abuse victim.

Living With Uncertainty and Unpredictability

CHRISTINA (COMMON EGO)

Your partner seems content, and then they fly into a rage for no apparent reason. What's going on here, and how can you self-regulate around someone who is so unpredictable?

Splitting: Dr. Jekyll or Mr. Hyde?

Most toxic people have what is often referred to as a Jekyll and Hyde personality, and this is especially true when you're dealing with a narcissist. Narcissists engage in what's called splitting, which means that you are either completely bad or completely good. And they treat you according to what they think at the moment.

Not only can this be extremely uncomfortable for their victims, but it creates intermittent reinforcement that leads to a trauma bond. As far as a narcissist is concerned, you're either an angel or a devil. There is very little in between.

Why the victim walks on eggshells

When you always have to be careful about what you say or do around someone for fear of setting them off, your behavior could be described as walking on eggshells.

If you're in a relationship with someone who is unpredictable and has a Jekyll and Hyde personality, you will inevitably find yourself walking on eggshells. This is because anything you say or do could potentially trigger their anger. And when they're angry, they may lash out at you. As such, you may find yourself tiptoeing around them, trying to avoid anything that might set them off.

It can be extremely difficult to live with someone who has a toxic personality. Not only are they unpredictable and volatile, but they also tend to drain the life out of those around them. If you're in a relationship with a narcissist or other type of toxic person, you may find yourself feeling exhausted, drained, and even depressed. You may also find it difficult to enjoy your own hobbies and interests outside of the relationship.

Why the victim is always seeking approval and validation from the abuser

The victim of a narcissist or other type of toxic person is always seeking approval and validation from the abuser. This is because they have been conditioned to believe that their worthiness and value as a human being depends on the approval of the abuser.

Narcissists in particular, are known for purposefully using manipulation and emotional blackmail to control their victims. They may make threats such as -

"If you don't do what I want, I'll leave you"

"If you don't give me what I want, I'll find someone else who will."

This kind of manipulative behavior can make the victim feel as though they are walking on eggshells, always needing to please the abuser in order to avoid their wrath.

Victims of emotional abuse often develop low self-esteem and lose self-confidence. They may also start to doubt their own judgment and reality. This is because the abuser has gaslighted them into believing that their thoughts, feelings, and perceptions are wrong or invalid. As such, they may find themselves constantly seeking approval from the abuser in an attempt to gain some semblance of control over their own lives.

What it's like living in a constant state of worry

You may find yourself constantly second-guessing your own thoughts and feelings, as well as trying to please the abuser in an attempt to avoid their anger or abuse. This takes a toll on your mental and emotional health, leaving you in a constant state of stress that can lead to physical health issues over time.

Chronic stress can lead to a number of physical and mental health problems, such as anxiety, depression, heart disease, stroke, and even death. When you're in a constant state of worry or stress, your body releases the hormone cortisol. This is known as the *"stress hormone"* because it helps your body to deal with stressful situations.

However, when cortisol levels remain high for extended

periods of time (as they do in cases of chronic stress), it can cause serious damage to your body. In severe cases, it can even lead to a form of post-traumatic stress disorder (PTSD).

If you're in a relationship like this, you may feel like you can handle it or you've got things under control, but it's important to consider the long-term effects this fear and uncertainty can have on you. This type of situation can be extremely damaging to your mental and emotional health, and it's important to get out of it before it causes irreparable damage.

Shame, Guilt & Denial in the Victim

DR. ANGEL J. STORM

Shame, guilt & denial are powerful states of belief that keep victims trapped in abusive relationships for years. When someone experiences abuse, they often feel like they are to blame for the situation, even though this is never the case. And to make matters worse, they may deny that the abuse is happening or has happened.

Unfortunately, the aftermath of that abuse can be a complicated emotional journey for the survivor. These powerful and complex emotions can be incredibly difficult to shake, and can lead to a range of negative consequences, such as depression, anxiety, and even post-traumatic stress disorder.

How shame, guilt and denial keep you trapped in abuse

Let's break down these feelings so that you can identify the root cause of all of them.

1. Shame

Shame will make you feel like you're not good enough for your abuser and that you're not doing enough for yourself or your family to get out of the situation you find yourself in. If you are in a relationship right now that you are feeling ashamed about, first ask yourself -

"If this was a relationship with anybody else, would I be responding the way I am right now?"

The reason this answer is so powerful to discover is because typically people have a belief around the relationship that is toxic and abusive. In other words, if it's a marriage, your belief structure might tell you that it's shameful to be divorced, that what you were experiencing is not actually abuse or that your abuser's actions don't warrant you leaving the marriage.

Perhaps you were raised in a home where abuse was taught or valued or perhaps you feel like you've messed up so many times that you can't bear to think about disappointing your family, community or yourself one more time.

2. Guilt

Guilt will make you feel like you're responsible for abuse. Guilt will often make you believe that there is something that you could be doing in your relationship with the abuser that would somehow cause them to stop being abusive.

Guilt will tell you that you're not smart enough to figure out what that one thing was, but if you were, all of these problems would go away. The toxic person will often use guilt in order to further trap their victims by convincing them that -

- No one else will love them
- They won't be able to survive without the abuser in their life
- They will never have a fulfilling life without the abuser

Why? Because ultimately you - the victim - are the problem.

3. Denial

Denial is a nice way of saying you are gaslighting yourself - you're denying what's actually happening in order to maintain an appearance. To hold on to hope that the version of your abuser that you have constructed in your mind could be real, or because the way out of the abuse seems too overwhelming to think about.

Denial is often done in response to feelings of shame and guilt. In other words, you may feel so shameful about your situation or feel so guilty for the role you are playing in the abusive relationship that you find yourself denying the reality of what is happening. It is easier to live out a make-believe life, then to change the one you are living.

Fear fuels shame, guilt and denial

All three of these (false) states of belief have fear at the root of them. If there was no more fear and if you knew you could not fail, you would be making a different decision. One of the ways to know if you are making the right choice for your life and for your family is to ask yourself this question:

"If someone was treating my child or my best friend this way, would I be okay with it or would I recommend they do something different?"

In abusive situations, the victim can become so molded to fit the abuser's preference of them that they lose sight of who they truly are and how to make decisions that line up with their true identity. This question can help put things in perspective immediately, and give you the strength to start making choices authentically and from a place of love instead of from a place of fear.

Psychological Consequences of Abuse in a Toxic Relationship

DR. ANGEL J. STORM

There is more education happening today about abuse, but there is still a misunderstanding that unless it is physical or sexual in nature, it isn't real or provable in court. Abuse is more than just physical violence and that emotional, verbal, financial and spiritual violence are just as damaging if not more so than physical violence.

If you recognize that you are experiencing one of these forms of abuse, please know that help is available and that you are not alone.

Emotional abuse can leave invisible scars

In a toxic relationship, the abuser will often use tactics such as verbal, emotional, financial and spiritual abuse to control and manipulate the victim without leaving any "*physical*" evidence of abuse on the victim. Yet, the victim will feel isolated, helpless and ashamed, which allows the abuse to escalate and continue.

As the abuse continues, victims will also start to doubt their own sanity and question their worth as a person. We know for a fact that the long-term effects of psychological abuse can be devastating to the physical, mental and financial states of the victim and can lead to depression, anxiety, and post-traumatic stress disorder (PTSD) or complex PTSD and even suicidality.

Maybe as you're reading these symptoms, you're identifying these thoughts as ones you have had. Maybe you are finding it difficult to trust people again and therefore you find yourself very isolated and feeling more and more like damaged goods or believing that your life will never improve.

Editor's Note

Emotional or psychological abuse, experienced in childhood or adulthood, can lead to several long-term and short-term mental health issues in the victim, such as –

- Chronic stress
- Anxiety disorders
- Depression
- Borderline personality disorder
- Post-traumatic stress disorder
- Social anxiety
- Eating disorders
- Substance use disorder
- Epigenetic changes
- Neuroticism (tendency to experience negative emotions)
- Attachment issues
- Insomnia
- Loneliness
- Apathy or emotional detachment & disconnect
- Changes in mood and behavior
- Self-injury or suicidality

When abuse is "invisible"

Victims of psychological abuse will typically be controlled through tactics such as intimidation, threats and destruction of property so that the victim continues to feel trapped and isolated. Specifically, when the abuse is "*invisible*," you may prolong reaching out for help because you don't feel that you have enough evidence for people to believe you or your side of the story. It is common that when you are dealing with a covert narcissist that they put on a facade in front of the rest of the world that does not line up with your experience or your testimony about this person.

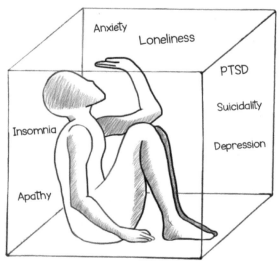

One of the most underreported and under-evaluated effects of psychological abuse is the loss of a victim's voice. It is very common that people who suffer this type of abuse do not report it or speak out about their reality and therefore they become more and more reliant on their abuser to do the right thing or to get the help that they need.

Strengthen your voice

Sharing your story, even if it's to yourself, is one of the most powerful ways that you can start undoing the psychological effects of abuse that you have endured. Strengthening your voice leads to a strengthening of identity.

As you use your voice to start telling your story, it undoes one by one the effects of abuse the toxic relationship has left on you. Sharing your story can lead you to finding a great support group, where you find out that you are not alone, and this can destroy the feeling of hopelessness, isolation, or the belief that no one will believe your side of the story.

Sharing your story in therapy can help you undo the effects of PTSD or C-PTSD and you can discover that there are ways to overcome the triggers, nightmares and memories of the abuse. You may even discover a way for your experience to serve you and others so that more people are set free from living in abusive relationships.

Learning to use your voice can also help you to advocate for yourself, even in healthy relationships, so that you understand how to set and enforce boundaries - and get comfortable doing so. Using your voice will help you start your journey of overcoming the prison the abuser has tried to keep you in for so long. It will reclaim your identity and increase your strength to heal and move forward with your dreams.

"Words will never hurt me."

The worst type of violence is making somebody feel like they are not worthy to be who they are. It destroys identities, purposes and family destinies. There used to be a rhyme children would say –

"Sticks and stones may break my bones but words will never hurt me."

That message is far from true. Bones can heal, bruises will fade, but the neural connections needed to make healthy decisions and live authentically need to be rebuilt with intention. Time does not make that happen automatically. Words shape realities. Words do hurt because they lead to a thought which leads to a belief.

If you are reading this and you find yourself in a non-physically violent situation, you need to realize that you are worthy of life. Hammer this point home: *The effects of psychological abuse can be just as damaging - if not more so - than physical abuse.*

Physical abuse tends to highlight the urgency of the need to get out of the relationship whereas verbal and emotional abuse tends to lead to the thinking that things aren't so bad and will change on their own, which prolongs the abuse and loss of identity. If you think you might be in a toxic relationship, reach out for help from a friend or family member or professional today.

Healing is possible

You deserve to be treated with respect and love. The abuse will not get better. Abuse increases the longer you stay because you *"get used to"* the first level of abuse and the abuser (like an addict) needs more control and power over you. The level of abuse you're experiencing today will be the least amount of abuse you will ever experience in that relationship.

The time to get out is now. You can escape. You do have options. Trust yourself and love yourself enough to pursue the pathway out of abuse and into freedom. If abuse is all you've ever known, meet with someone you trust who can help you walk out your escape plan. Take deliberate steps to break the trauma bond once and for all and fill your life up with love and hope.

Emotional Consequences of Abuse in a Toxic Relationship

SIGNE M. HEGESTAND

It's not always easy to talk about the emotional impact of abuse, especially when you have been at the receiving end. Being exposed to emotional abuse, whether as a child or an adult, can wreak havoc on your mental and emotional well-being. The toxic relationship blatantly destroys the basic experiences of security and trust and leads to painful emotional experiences with a lack of empathy, compassion and care.

Impact of experiencing abuse in childhood

Growing up in a toxic, dysfunctional home can lead to severe and fundamental damage in a child that can affect their mindset, personality, self-esteem, attachment style, ability to regulate emotions and adult relationships. If you have grown up with childhood emotional abuse, neglect and maltreatment, you may have had difficulty growing up as a child, resulting in attachment disorders, chronic stress, anxiety, depression, post-traumatic stress disorder (PTSD), loneliness and hopelessness.

When a child experiences a high degree of insecurity in an emotionally abusive environment, they are likely to develop an insecure attachment style as an adult. You may become very clingy and afraid of being abandoned due to your insecurities. Or you may avoid close relationships and cut yourself off from the outside world.

Experiencing abuse and trauma in early life can also lead to

155

developmental problems, such as learning difficulties & behavioral issues, and psychopathology such as Borderline & Antisocial Personality Disorders. Childhood abuse can also affect cognitive development and academic performance, which may further add to learning difficulties.

When you are exposed to psychological or emotional abuse, you not only lose your basic trust and confidence in other people, but also *in yourself.*

Impact of experiencing abuse in adulthood

Being exposed to emotional abuse as an adult can also have a severe and long-lasting impact on your mental well-being, leading to chronic stress, anxiety, depression, PTSD, overwhelming thoughts, low self-esteem and self-doubt. If you have experienced abuse in your adult relationships, whether romantic or otherwise, you may also experience physical symptoms such as chronic pain, headaches, and digestive issues.

Abuse can leave you in a constant state of fight-or-flight, making you end up in a chronic burnout state. This can negatively affect your ability to work productively and significantly decrease your quality of life. Abused adults also have difficulty forming and maintaining healthy relationships, and they may struggle with trust and intimacy issues. They may also turn to unhealthy coping mechanisms such as substance abuse, self-harm and suicidal ideation.

The insecurity, the control and the unpredictability of the toxic relationship can also make you easily anxious or triggered by normal everyday experiences such as the sound of a text message. Even the smallest reminders of your past abusive relationship can trigger an anxiety attack.

In the worst-case scenario, you may be so traumatized by the abuse that you develop Complex Post Traumatic Stress Disorder (C-PTSD), which is a more complex and pervasive form of PTSD. You are more likely to develop C-PTSD if you experienced childhood abuse as well, since the traumas that trigger this disorder are not a single incident, but are long-term and repeated traumatic experiences. However, the impact can vary depending on the type and duration of abuse, as well as the victim's resilience and coping mechanisms.

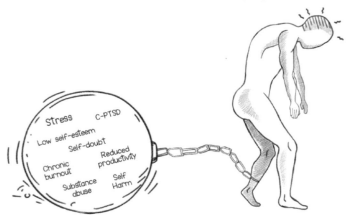

When abuse leads to trauma

Emotional abuse, whether experienced in childhood or adulthood, can lead to trauma in some cases. Moreover, survivors of emotional abuse may struggle with feelings of shame, guilt, and self-blame, which can contribute to the development of complex post-traumatic stress disorder (C-PTSD). In fact, research shows that emotional abuse, rather than both physical and sexual abuse, was the biggest risk factor for developing PTSD and C-PTSD. It can make you struggle with regulating your emotions and forming close relationships due to feelings of low self-worth, guilt and shame.

Trauma can even affect your ability to function in daily life, whether at your job or in your home. You may find it difficult to develop an intimate relationship with someone and have the confidence that another person can love and support you unconditionally.

The belittling, critical and devaluing behavior that your toxic partner, family member or friend has exposed you to can also result in long-term stress, anxiety or depression. You may experience a lack of zest for life, have difficulty sleeping and negative thoughts that run-in circles (rumination).

To lose oneself

One of the most painful consequences of abuse is the deep experience of having lost yourself. The manipulation and breakdown you have been exposed to causes you to experience self-doubt and confusion about your own inner experiences and feelings. You feel like your inner compass is broken and needs to be recalibrated.

In addition, sadness and self-harming behavior can also often appear even after you have walked away from the toxic relationship, which to the outside world can seem illogical. But to you the relationship mattered. You have lost love, trust, dreams, hopes and desires for your life. You have lost a lot – yourself, perhaps your home, work, money, your relationship and life partner, and in extreme cases your children. Your self-understanding may have changed significantly.

However, this grief is somewhat more complex, as you will often have many ambivalent feelings and experiences. Looking at these losses and giving them space, as you would in any other grieving process, can be a valuable development opportunity.

It is important to note that every individual's experience with abuse is unique, and the effects of childhood abuse can vary widely depending on the type, frequency, and severity of the abuse. Receiving the right trauma-informed treatment and support can help you manage and overcome these effects gradually.

Social Consequences of Abuse on Victims of Toxic Relationships

DR. MARIETTE JANSEN

Humans are social animals and social interaction is a necessity. They need others to survive when young and to thrive when older. However, when someone is subjected to emotional abuse, social interaction will not help them thrive as the victim is focused on accommodating and conflict-avoiding.

How abuse affects our social behavior

There are two input areas that affect someone's social behavior:

1. How they see themselves?
2. How they see others?

Let us understand why these two key areas are important.

1. **How they see themselves**

   - **No sense of self:** No knowledge on who they are, what they want, what makes them special and different.
   - **No confidence:** The abuser will have chipped away on any self-belief, self-confidence and trust the victim had in themselves.
   - **Self-doubt:** As the abuser has blamed the victim for everything, the first thought when something goes wrong will be '*What have I done wrong?*'
   - **No internal validation:** The victim doesn't trust

their own opinions as they have always been challenged and instead look at other people for confirmation (external validation).

- **No self-worth:** Not used to being treated nicely, the victim will do anything for kindness.

In a social context, you can recognize a victim through their shyness. They will stay in the background and try to blend in. Or even better, being invisible. They find it difficult to speak about them and if you ask them a direct question they will flutter and struggle for words.

When there is an interaction, they might ask you what you think as they don't have their own opinion. If you are kind to them, they might cling onto you and give the *'relationship'* way more value than is justified.

2. **How they deal with others**

- **Others are better than me:** There is the tendency to look up to others.
- **Others know better than me:** There is the need to

follow others in what they say or do.

- **I take the blame when something goes wrong and feel the need to make it better:** They display typical *'rescuer'* behavior.

- **Others can make me feel better about myself:** *"When they validate me or my ideas, I will feel good about myself."* However, that doesn't last long as the self-doubt will kick in, leading to anxiety, stress and rumination.

- **Kindness needs to be rewarded:** *'I do anything for kindness'* and will create another opportunity to be abused.

- **Difficulty with boundaries:** Both setting them and recognizing them. This easily leads to uncomfortable situations.

Abuse corrupts social relationships

It is difficult to build a healthy relationship with a victim of emotional abuse. Healthy connections are about respect, balance and exchange. A victim, however, will be more drawn towards toxic, codependent relationships as they look up to others. They will never see themselves at the same level as you and give you more credit than you actually deserve.

They also try to salvage situations, even if they have nothing to do with it. It can be really irritating, when someone tries to rescue another when it is none of their business. However, the reality is they are deeply hurt and are only trying to help someone else to experience a glimmer of hope they need themselves.

Valuing others more than self

Another imbalance comes up when the victim feels treated with kindness. You give them attention, listen to them or just compliment them and they will feel obliged to give back to you. Maybe by buying all the drinks or running errands for you. It might feel uncomfortable, as their rewards are over the top and show how much more they value you than themselves.

There is the big issue around boundaries, which separate someone's physical and emotional space, feelings, needs and responsibilities. Healthy people draw lines, which define what is acceptable behavior towards them and are able to communicate these assertively. It helps to keep relationships healthy and respectful.

Victims of abuse have no sense of self and easily morph into someone else and their needs. They are incapable of setting boundaries and setting themselves up to be taken advantage of, violated and abused.

Lack of boundaries can lead to the following patterns:

1. **Codependency:** They are identifying themselves with someone else. They are mirroring their partner or friend's feelings *'If he is happy, I am happy'*, they speak in *'we'* language instead of *'I'* and they keep themselves dependent on each other.

2. **Being a doormat:** Because a victim doesn't say *'stop, this is enough'* they might find themselves being treated with disrespect and exploitation.

3. **Feeling rejected:** Victims don't understand boundaries and easily overstep those of others by acting inappropriately. Then they feel misunderstood and rejected.

4. **Highly anxious:** Walking on 'eggshells', lacking knowledge about what is right and wrong causes high levels of stress and anxiety.

Self-awareness is the key to healthier connections

Emotional abuse impacts the very ideas of how victims see themselves, which impacts the way they interact with others. Healthy and balanced relationships are impossible until the victim has become self-aware and values who they are.

Self-knowledge, acceptance and self-love will feed how they then relate to others. Not from a perspective of being less important, valuable and loveable but from a perspective of self-respect, applying boundaries and the wish to build balanced relationships and equal interactions.

Evaluating Your Own Experience of Abuse

DR. MARIETTE JANSEN

I never knew until I reached 55.

"How come someone intelligent like me has been so stupid?"

I have heard these words from lots of victims of narcissistic abuse in my therapy room. And they apply to me as well - a trained psychotherapist, self-aware and helping others with their emotional struggles, who had no clue how dysfunctional and damaging her upbringing was.

What happened to me, and to others in similar circumstances, is that you are brainwashed by your abuser. You are put down, neglected, exploited, and emotionally abused. You will be blamed for everything that goes wrong and made responsible as your abusers don't take any responsibility. Unless, it is something that will make them look good. You will never get the credits for anything.

From childhood, all victims miss out on healthy emotional and mental development. The focus of life is on surviving, the actions are about pleasing the narcissist and there is no scope for focus on themselves.

My journey of self-discovery

I never felt happy in our family, and thought it was me. However, when I started therapy at the age of 27, I discovered it had all to do with my mother. Knowing my issues were related to my mother made me focus on her. But I was the one who put in the effort, time and money, while she was sitting back blaming me for the failure of our relationship.

Looking back, I can see how I repeated patterns with boyfriends, who treated me as badly as she did. But through therapy I started to build more personal awareness and confidence. Yet, my mother was able to shatter me instantly. I wasn't able to change her strong negative effect on me.

A breakthrough moment was offered by Google, through a checklist on NPD. My mother ticked all the boxes and it changed my perspective. With knowledge about her personality disorder, I tried to manage our interactions differently, but she could still bring me to tears with one single remark. The main breakthrough was the moment I gave up hope. Hope that she can give me something positive. No hope for any change meant that I could go '*no contact*', which gave me peace. At last.

My role in the abuse

Emotional abuse between two people becomes a reality via transactions between the abuser (my narcissist mother) and me, the enabler and victim. If the target (potential victim) doesn't emotionally engage, they don't enable and can keep themselves safe. Only when the enabler is aware of their role and behavior are they able to turn their position from victim to victor.

Stepping stones to change

1. **Focus on yourself and how you are affected by them.** If you are abused, you are most likely empathic and focus on the abuser. That is how they get you and how you keep yourself in their grip. Don't think about the abuser, their reasons, '*how can they do this?*' and '*why?*'.

2. **You will never understand your abuser.** You might as well stop trying to comprehend their actions and thoughts.

3. **Acknowledge and own your feelings.** Allow yourself to be angry and upset, but only at certain times. This is your *"child position"* and if you stay too long in it, you won't step into your power.

4. **Find ways of keeping yourself safe.** I decided to talk to my mother on the phone once a fortnight for 20 minutes. I had also made a list of *'forbidden'* subjects, knowing how upsetting they were.

5. **Put yourself first.** If you are not feeling strong, stay away from your abuser, because they will get at you. In my case, I cut her out of my life, when I was 59 and she was 86. One of the best things I have ever done.

6. **Stop the guilt.** Emotional abuse always creates guilt (Unhealthy Guilt Syndrome), because you have been blamed and told you got it wrong. And doing something wrong evokes the natural feeling of guilt. However, as a victim you haven't done anything wrong.

7. **Watch out for the moralists.** A lot of people embrace the Walt Disney fairy tale, that a mother loves her child or that she doesn't mean it. It is too painful for them to see the reality, but you know your reality. And as a victim it is harsh and tough.

8. **Don't justify your choices to others.** If you know what works for you, just do it. People who don't share your abusive experiences will never understand the pain. My good friend kept shaking her head about my mother, saying she couldn't imagine a mother acting like that as she had a very loving mum.

9. **You didn't choose to be in this position.** It is what you are being exposed to, but it is not your fault.

However, you can change the abusive situation by stopping to be an enabler through getting more knowledge and learning skills.

Abuse is a great mentor

I have my mother a lot to thank for. Not for what she directly gave to me, but how she forced me to travel my journey. I had to make hard and harsh choices, like cutting her out and giving up all hope for a decent relationship. I learned how not everything in life can be repaired and sometimes accepting is the only way forward. I know that life isn't fair. But that we all are more powerful once we learn to step into our power.

I learned to be empathetic with others without losing myself. To put boundaries in place and keep myself safe. And above all, I learned I am a good person, who is responsible for her own happiness.

That is a great gift from my darling mother.

Editor's Note

Importance of analyzing abuse

Reflecting on your experiences of abuse can often be triggering and traumatizing as you mentally relive the moments of abuse. However, it is a crucial step in the healing process as it helps you understand all the red flags you missed, the factors that led to the abuse, the manipulation strategies used by the toxic person and what you can do to transform your situation.

It is common for most of us to repress our memories of abuse, to deny or minimize our experiences and normalize toxic relationships. However, this can take a serious toll on our physical, mental, emotional and spiritual health. Acknowledging the abuse will enable you to gain a clear understanding of your reality and identify the fact that you are the victim, not the perpetrator despite how your abuser may want to present it.

Analysis, acknowledgment and self-reflection is the first step towards healing from the trauma of abuse. But healing never comes easy. It will only come to you when you face difficult thoughts and emotions and go where you don't want to - the truth of your reality. Accepting that you are in an abusive relationship, sorting your thoughts, remembering crucial details and addressing your genuine emotions will help you unlearn toxic patterns and develop healthy patterns of thoughts and behaviors.

It will allow you to gain clarity about your past and present, practice self-love and self-compassion and progress in your healing journey.

How to analyze your experience of abuse?

You can start acknowledging your reality by asking yourself questions like -

"At what point did my relationship start to turn toxic?"

"How has the abuse affected me and my relationship?"

"Has the experience changed my thoughts and behaviors?"

"What can I do now to make things better for myself?"

"Is there any way for me to fix the relationship or is it better to leave?"

"Who can I ask for help? Should I consult a professional therapist?"

Facing the truth by uncovering your insecurities, shame, regrets, fears and guilt can be extremely challenging. It will take a lot of inner strength for you to move through this process. And once you go through the challenging steps, you will start healing. However, healing can be a time-consuming process and it may take months or years for you to completely heal from the trauma of abuse.

Prioritize yourself

While trauma can be a curse from your abuser, healing is a gift you give yourself. However, analysis, acknowledgment and self-reflection is a continuous process that you need practice even after you think you have healed. Abuse can leave deep scars in our mind, heart and soul and acknowledgement can help us build a healthier life that is sustainable.

Acceptance is the only way to be your most genuine self - flawed and glorious, irrespective of what stage of healing you are in.

CHAPTER FOUR

THE GAME OF ABUSE

UNDERSTANDING ABUSE IN TOXIC RELATIONSHIPS

Toxicity vs. Abuse

LINDA GREYMAN

Many people use the terms "toxic" and "abusive" to describe unhealthy relationships interchangeably. However, there are subtle differences between both terms even though they are related. While both the terms help to classify unhealthy & damaging relationships, whether romantic or otherwise, the distinction is often vague even for the individuals involved in such relationships.

Although all abusive relationships are toxic, all toxic relationships are not abusive. Both toxic & abusive behavior lies on a spectrum and several factors, such as intention and repetition of behavior, tend to determine how unhealthy and damaging a relationship is.

Toxic behavior vs abusive behavior

When negative behavior occurs as an isolated incident, it may not necessarily be toxic. However, if such behavior becomes repetitive even after they have been communicated about their bitterness, then it can be toxic. And when such toxic behavior is done intentionally to harm the other person, then it becomes abusive.

Toxic people often behave the way they do due to certain mental health issues such as personality disorders or cognitive biases. It is just the way they are. But abusive people make a conscious decision to hurt others through damaging actions and behavior. Toxic behavior is born out of a lack of control while abusive behavior is an attempt by the abuser to take control of the relationship and the other person.

Understanding what exactly toxic and abusive relationships

consist of can enable us to figure out the subtle differences between toxicity and abuse.

What makes a relationship toxic

Most people in relationships argue and fight, but toxic relationships are tainted with criticism, desperation, insecurity, devaluation and threats. It is characterized by a lack of support, dishonesty, jealousy and bitterness. It involves cycles of disproportionate behaviors, actions and reactions by one or both partners.

When one person behaves in a toxic manner, the other person typically reacts in a controlled and positive manner. When both people are toxic, they will equally respond in a negative way and overreact to problems, blaming each other. While toxic romantic relationships can result in emotional disconnection, it can also make one of both partners codependent due insecure attachment.

In a toxic relationship, the following typically exists -

- Needs of one person is ignored by the other
- Relational issues are left unresolved
- Lack of open and honest communication
- Unnecessary drama
- Lack of accountability or blame shifting
- Lack or violation of healthy personal boundaries

Toxic relationships can leave you feeling drained and unhappy and drastically lower your self-esteem. Instead of outright abusive behavior, it is often filled with passive-aggressive behavior, criticisms, sarcasm and insults.

Toxic Behviour
(Born out of lack of control)

Abusive Behviour
(An attempt to take control)

What makes a relationship abusive

Although toxicity arises out of a lack of control, abuse manifests out of a need for control. When toxic behavior is colored by control and deliberately becomes more damaging and threatening, it turns into abuse. An abusive relationship involves disrespect, threats, aggression and violence that can lead to harm or damage. The primary objective of abuse, whether physical, sexual, verbal or emotional, is to gain power and control over another person.

Abuse typically starts as toxic behavior and escalates over time turning violent and harmful. Apart from physical violence, abuse may also involve coercion, isolation, intimidation, controlling behavior etc.

Abusive relationships are usually characterized by -

- Physical and/or sexual violence
- Manipulation and control
- Angry outbursts
- Dominant behavior like aggression, intimidation & coercion
- Jealousy
- Gaslighting

Unlike toxic people, abusive people are always in control of their behaviors and are deliberate about their actions.

- Physical and sexual abuse is aimed to control the victim's willpower & body and to gain power over them.
- Emotional abuse is deliberately done to destroy the victim's confidence and to make them more compliant.
- Financial abuse helps to control the lifestyle of the victim.
- Gaslighting (psychological manipulation causing self-doubt) is an intentional action to control the victim's sense of sanity.
- Emotional abuse controls how the victim experiences life and how they see or define their existence.

Judy's Story

Backdrop:

Dane and Judy have been together for a year. Initially, their relationship was filled with love, admiration, and mutual respect. However, over time, they started feeling unsatisfied and unfulfilled in the relationship.

While Dane got a recent promotion at work, he started being more and more involved in work and less present to Judy. Judy on the other hand is now struggling single handedly to balance work life and household chores. She tries to bring attention to her unmet needs.

Let's see how Dane reacts to Judy, depending on whether the relationship is toxic or abusive.

➢ **In a toxic relationship scenario:**

When Judy asks for help with household chores, Dane may react negatively, saying something like, *"I work harder and longer hours than you, I make more money than you, so you should think harder before asking me to do chores. I've already had a bad day."*

In another instance, when Judy starts to complain about repeated arguments, Dane may react by saying, *"Oh, here we go again. It's always my fault, isn't it? You never take responsibility for anything. You're never satisfied, no matter what I do. I don't even know why I bother trying anymore."*

Whenever Judy protests about Dane's negative reactions, he may retaliate by saying, *"Judy, why are you always so sensitive? I can never do anything right in your eyes. Nothing I do is ever enough for you. Maybe if you didn't nag me all the time, we wouldn't have these constant arguments."*

Their conversations may turn into arguments, often triggered by trivial matters. Disappointments turn into resentment. Encouragement is replaced by criticism and social gatherings may become opportunities for creating drama. Their relationship is destroyed by their own disproportionate responses, toxic behaviors and competitiveness.

Although both Dane and Judy are aware of the negative impact their relationship is having on their well-being, they struggle to break free from the toxic cycle. They may find it difficult to communicate their needs, resulting in unresolved conflicts. Both partners are emotionally drained and feel trapped in an unhealthy dynamic.

> ➤ **In an abusive relationship scenario:**

When Judy asks for help with household chores, Dane may react abusively, saying, *"Do I need to remind you who you are talking to? It seems your memory fades as soon as your bruises heal. Maybe another black eye will knock some sense into you."*

In another instance, when Judy starts to set boundaries and asks Dane to treat her with respect, Dane may react by saying, *"Shut up! You know you're lucky to have me. No one else would put up with you. I'll do whatever it takes to keep you in line. And you'll regret it if you ever try to leave me. I'll make sure of it."*

Whenever Judy protests about Dane's control over her, he may react by saying, *"You're mine, Judy. I have the right to know where you are and who you're with at all times. I can't trust you because you're always lying and trying to hide things from me. You're nothing without me, Judy. You'll never be able to escape. I'll ruin your life if you ever try to escape."*

Every time Judy reacts to defend herself, Dane may physically abuse her by shoving, slapping, kicking and choking her. He may deliberately hit her on weekends instead of weekdays to make sure her colleagues don't see the bruises. When he can't hit her directly, he may kick and punch objects and walls to make his point clear.

He may even threaten her with suicide to maintain his control and keep her from leaving him. He may hide her passport and other documents away and remove her access from bank accounts making her feel powerless and helpless.

As the relationship becomes increasingly abusive, Dane becomes even more controlling, isolating Judy from her friends and family. He may monitor her every move, and criticize her appearance and choices.

Dane's behavior may get worse leading to episodes of physical violence, leaving Judy feeling frightened, helpless and trapped.

The above case example highlights the significant differences between a toxic *relationship and an abusive relationship, despite the underlying similarities in the scenario. While a toxic relationship can be emotionally draining and detrimental to well-being, an abusive relationship involves a power imbalance, fear, and potential physical harm.*

Toxicity can become abuse

Arguments and disagreements occur in every relationship no matter how healthy it may be. But people in healthy relationships sort their issues through communication, empathy and understanding.

Toxic relationships, however, lack communication which leads to disproportionate responses, like shouting and screaming, and an unbalanced relationship dynamic. Abusive partners, on the other hand, calmly calculate a course of action that will help them gain control over the other person through violence and manipulation.

Toxicity leaves you feeling drained and bitter. Abuse leaves you feeling confused and broken. However, the distinction between toxicity and abuse is too fine to be differentiated clearly. But the most crucial aspect to remember is that toxicity is driven by a lack of control, whereas abuse is driven by a need to control the other.

Both toxic and abusive behaviors in relationships are unhealthy and damaging, and hence, unacceptable as both can lead to serious mental and emotional health issues in the long run.

Types of Abuse

LINDA GREYMAN

What are the types of abuse? Well, there is only one type of abuse - the one that destroys you. The one that is vile and horrid. The one that no one should ever experience. The one that is unacceptable. The one that no one deserves. The abuse that insults your love and breaks your heart.

In toxic relationships, abuse can manifest in different ways and destroy someone, physically, mentally, emotionally and spiritually.

Types of Abuse

179

THE GAME OF ABUSE

The rotten core of abuse is pregnant with the desperate need for power and control. While most people think of physical violence when they hear the term abuse, it is a repeated pattern of behavior which can be materialized in a number of different ways.

Let's talk about some of the most common types of abuse that can unfortunately occur in toxic relationships.

1. Physical abuse

Physical abuse refers to intentional use of physical force and violence that can lead to physical harm, injuries, disability and even death. It can also involve physically forcing someone to do something against their will, such as taking drugs, or preventing them from accessing necessary utilities like food and medicines.

Physical violence is often used to make the victim more compliant by instilling fear of harm in them.

Physical abuse can include –

- Hitting, kicking, punching, slapping, biting, hair-pulling or pushing
- Manhandling
- Strangulation
- Burning
- Physical punishments
- Refusing utilities or coercing substance use
- Unauthorized restraint
- Damaging personal property
- Forcing someone to be physically uncomfortable or unsafe.

2. Emotional abuse

Also known as mental or psychological abuse, emotional

abuse is aimed at breaking the victim's self-esteem, sense of self-worth and self-confidence. This type of abuse is mostly subtle where the victim is unaware that they are being abused. As it can be both verbal and non-verbal, emotional abuse can have lasting and deep effects and make the victim feel broken and exhausted.

Emotional abuse can involve a wide array of psychological strategies such as -

- Manipulation
- Gaslighting or lying
- Humiliation, shaming, criticism and name-calling
- Enforced isolation
- Blame shifting
- Intimidation & threats
- Controlling victim's actions & behaviors
- Failure to respect boundaries & privacy
- Cyber bullying
- Silent treatment, ignoring or threats of abandonment.

3. Sexual abuse

Forcing a partner to have any unwanted sexual contact, even in a romantic relationship, is known as sexual abuse. While it typically involves nonconsensual or forced sexual activity, degrading or unsafe sexual practices even when it is consensual can be identified as sexual abuse.

Sexual abuse is more about power and control than about the act of having sex. It can involve different types of forced or unwanted sexual activities such as –

- Rape, attempted rape or sexual assault
- Sexual harassment

- Unwanted or inappropriate touching
- Coerced sexual acts, nudity or explicit photography
- Forced to watch pornography or sexual acts
- Non-consensual masturbation
- Indecent exposure
- Forced prostitution or human trafficking
- Engaging in sexual acts when the victim is not completely conscious
- Physically hurting the victim during sex

In case of minors, pregnancy can also be a sign and outcome of sexual abuse.

4. Verbal abuse

Verbal abuse is the use of words as weapons to destroy someone's self-esteem. The abuser may also use written texts, body language, facial expressions or other nonverbal cues to degrade and devalue the victim. It is perhaps the subtlest form of abuse in any relationship.

Verbal abuse uses negative statements or nonverbal reactions to make the victim feel unloved and unworthy. It may typically include -

- Name-calling
- Persistent insults, sarcasm and criticisms
- Hurtful comments disguised as jokes
- Silent treatment or sulking
- Minimizing or trivializing the victim's opinions
- Shouting or screaming at the victim, in public or private
- Sending derogatory messages through emails, texts or social media
- Refusing to listen

- Denial of truth
- Blame shifting or making false accusations

5. Financial abuse

Also known as economic or material abuse, it involves intentionally controlling the victim's finances. The abuser can withhold, take or misuse the victim's money, property, assets, materials, belongings or other resources for personal gain or to prevent the victim from accessing it through deception, threats or coercion.

The main goal of financial abuse is to control the victim and to make them financially dependent on the abuser. Some common examples of this form of abuse includes -

- Controlling financial assets and giving "allowance" to the victim
- Intentionally affecting the victim's credit score
- Preventing the victim from accessing their own assets or finances
- Controlling the victim's bank accounts
- Physically hurting the victim to prevent them from working
- Harassing the victim at workplace to tarnish their professional reputation
- Fraud, scam or theft of resources
- Exploiting the victim's finances or assets
- Taking loans or running debts in the victim's name
- Misuse of legal authority, like power of attorney etc.

6. Spiritual abuse

Alternatively known as intellectual abuse, it refers to abusive behaviors targeted at controlling the victim's religious / spiritual beliefs and intellectual interests. It can also involve the abuser using the victim's intellectual or spiritual beliefs to control, dominate or manipulate the victim.

Spiritual abuse can be extremely subtle as it primarily focuses on a specific belief system or religion that the victim pursues. This can include –

- Forcing the victim to go against their beliefs
- Punishing the victim for having different beliefs
- Preventing the victim from participating in certain spiritual practices
- Ridiculing or insulting the victim's beliefs and opinions
- Using the victim's beliefs to manipulate them
- Denying access to places of worship, rituals & ceremonies
- Forcing certain religions and faith on children
- Using spiritual and religious beliefs as an excuse for aggression and abuse
- Honor killing or harm
- Forcing to get married in the name of religion or culture.

Other forms of abuse in a toxic relationship

Apart from the ones stated above, a toxic relationship can involve many other types of abuse such as –

1. Digital abuse (online harassment & control through technology)
2. Cultural abuse (exploitation of cultural practices and traditions)
3. Discriminatory abuse (prejudice-based mistreatment due to differences)
4. Neglect (failure to care or pay attention)

5. Exploitation (Unfair use for personal gain)
6. Bullying (harmful behavior causing pain & intimidation)
7. Abandonment (loss, rejection, isolation, emptiness, longing, pain)
8. Stalking (Unwanted pursuit, intrusive obsession, unwavering presence)
9. Modern slavery (forced labor & domestic servitude)

Abuse is never acceptable

Abuse can be experienced by anyone regardless of their age or sex. You should always remember that no matter what, abuse should never be tolerated or accepted. It is NOT your fault. You do NOT deserve it. Make sure to seek help and support, if you or someone you know is experiencing abuse in a toxic relationship. You can seek help from local authorities, medical professionals, local abuse hotlines or a trusted loved one.

Remember, help is always available and you are never alone.

Stages of Abuse
in a Toxic Relationship

LINDA GREYMAN

Abuse never starts right off the bat. It builds slowly over time. The abuser sizes up the victim like a predator stalks its prey. They move in slowly one step at a time. One stage at a time. And when they have the target locked on the victim; they move in for the kill. Whether it's for the predator or the abuser, the game is the same. Hide, stalk, deceive, bait, tempt, hunt, annihilate, and satisfy your hunger for power, control and narcissistic supply.

Abuse progresses in phases and stages. Understanding the different stages of abuse involved in a toxic relationship can help you identify a potential abuser and protect yourself.

Stages in the cycle of abuse

The cycle of abuse is mainly a recurring pattern of abusive behavior observed in toxic relationships. The cycle involves four primary stages which repeats itself once a cycle ends. This cyclic repetition of abuse stems from power imbalances and insecure attachments in toxic relationships.

Every relationship, no matter how unhealthy, typically starts in a healthy, positive way full of love, passion, support and appreciation. Toxic relationships, however, start as a game with the toxic person preying on unsuspecting potential victims. These predators draw in their prey through manipulation tactics like paying excessive attention, love bombing etc. And once the prey is hooked, the toxic person starts toying with the victim using an arsenal of psychological manipulation tactics to control and dominate them.

This is why a toxic relationship turns sour as it progresses through four distinct steps –

1. Tension Building Stage

Once the relationship has been established and the abuser has the victim in their grasp, the reality of the abuser starts to creep in. Minor conflicts and arguments start taking place frequently. The abuser increasingly becomes more demanding, critical, dominant and controlling.

The abuser starts taking out their frustration of external stressors on the victim by acting insecure, anxious, paranoid or even aggressive. The victim becomes confused and accommodates the abusers' toxic behaviors due to their inherent people pleasing tendencies.

After all, the victim wants to try harder to make the relationship work. This encourages the abuser to violate the victim's boundaries further. As the toxic person becomes more abusive, the victim becomes more anxious, alert and cautious around the abuser.

2. Incident of Abuse Stage

This stage is marked by a sudden eruption of abusive behavior from the abuser towards the victim. When the tension becomes extreme, the abuser releases it through violent outbursts or abusive behavior. Such behavior can manifest in various forms, such as physical violence, emotional manipulation, verbal assaults, or sexual coercion.

The victim is subjected to the abuser's rage, cruelty, and disregard for their well-being. The abuser may, ironically, pretend to be the victim and shift the blame of their toxic behavior on the non-toxic person.

This stage often leaves the victim feeling trapped, frightened, and emotionally wounded, while the abuser gains a sense of power and control. The incident of abuse serves as a painful reminder of the toxic dynamics at play in the relationship and the destructive impact it has on the victim's physical and emotional safety.

3. Reconciliation Stage

Following the incident of abuse, the reconciliation stage emerges, offering a glimmer of hope for resolution and change within the relationship. This stage typically occurs after a certain period of time has passed since the last stage.

Once things have cooled down and the abuser has let off some steam, they may regret their abusive behavior and feel guilty. So, when the tension finally starts to reduce, the abuser may admit that they made a mistake, apologize to the victim and promise to improve.

However, without genuine and lasting change, the abuser's apologies and gestures of remorse can be deceptive and designed to maintain control over the victim. Their regret and apology can simply be a calculated step to keep the victim from leaving. Abusers are experts in playing mind games and manipulating people. The abuser will apologize only to make the victim feel safe, secure, reassured and hopeful for their future together.

This stage also involves love-bombing, where the abuser showers the victim with attention, affection, praise, gifts and surprises in an attempt to mimic the initial "honeymoon phase" that exists in all romantic relationships where everything feels great and perfect.

4. Calm Stage

The calm before the storm. However, it is important to recognize that the calm stage is typically a temporary respite within the cycle of abuse. The underlying issues that contribute to the toxic dynamics of the relationship still remains unresolved, and the potential for future abusive incidents lingers.

This is the stage where everything feels peaceful but underneath it all, the tension is starting to simmer again, signaling the start of a new abuse cycle. However, the abuser will remain charming, loving and attentive during this stage. But instead of being apologetic, they will come up with more excuses and justifications for their behaviors and actions.

While the abuser may still apologize, they will find something to shift the blame on. They may apologize, but with justifications. The abuser may even minimize the victim's experience of abuse by gaslighting them. While the abuser may try to shift blame, they will still be regretful & ashamed and promise to make things right. The victim is likely to trust the abuser's false promises, and put their guards down. The abuser will continue to be loving and caring during this stage but this calmness will not last for long. It is crucial for the victim to remain vigilant and aware of the warning signs, as the calm stage often serves as a precursor to the tension building stage and the subsequent recurrence of abuse.

The relationship will move back to the 'tension building' stage all over again where tensions will start to arise from the cracks once more.

SARAH'S STORY

Sarah and Mark had been dating for two years and seemed like the perfect couple to those around them.

However, behind closed doors, their relationship was anything but healthy. The stages of abuse emerged gradually, as outlined below:

Tension building

During this stage, tension and unease start to build within the relationship. Minor conflicts, misunderstandings, and disagreements become more frequent due to Mark's possessiveness and need for control. Sarah felt like she was walking on eggshells, anxious about triggering Mark's anger.

Mark: *"Hey, who are you texting so often? It seems like you're always glued to your phone."*

Sarah: *"Oh, it's just a friend. We're catching up on some things. Is there a problem?"*

Mark: *"Well, it's just that you've been texting this person a lot lately. Are you sure it's just a friend? I don't want you to text him so often."*

Sarah: *"Trust me, there's nothing to worry about."*

Incident of abuse stage

This stage was characterized by intense arguments, verbal insults, and, at times, physical aggression from Mark. Sarah became the primary target of Mark's anger, enduring emotional and physical harm during these outbursts.

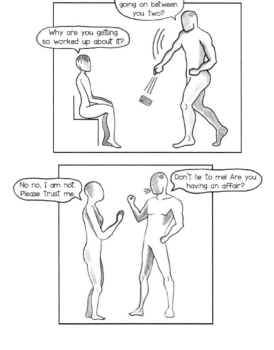

Mark: *"Is there something going on between you and that person?"*

Sarah: *"It's just a friend, seriously. Why are you getting so worked up about it?"*

Mark: *"Don't lie to me! I saw the way you were smiling while talking to him. I won't tolerate this anymore! Are you cheating on me?"*

Sarah: *"No no, I am not. Please trust me. I will never talk to him if you say so. Please don't hurt me."*

Reconciliation

During this stage, Mark would express remorse after each explosive episode, promising that he would change and seek help. Sarah, hopeful for a better future, would believe his apologies and give him another chance.

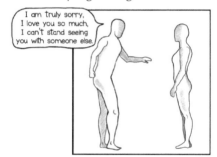

Mark: *"I am truly sorry; I shouldn't let my jealousy consume me. I love you so much, I can't stand seeing you with someone else. I trust you, and I need to remind myself of that. In the future I promise to talk about it instead of letting it fester."*

Sarah: *"I'm glad we're on the same page. We're a team, and we can handle any challenges that come us way."*

Calm

This phase was marked by Mark's excessive displays of attention, affection, gifts, and gestures of reconciliation. Sarah felt relieved and hopeful, believing that the abuse was finally over.

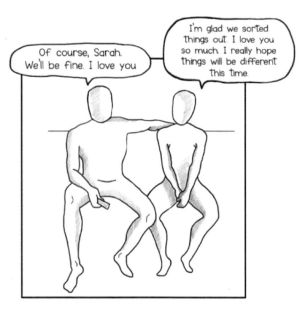

Mark: *"I'm really sorry about our fight earlier. I didn't mean to say those things. I love you so much. Can we start fresh? Please?"*

Sarah: *"I appreciate you saying that. I love you more than words can express. I'm sorry too. I will be more careful about my actions from now on."*

However, as abuse occurs in a repetitive pattern, such toxic behaviors can occur again and again, even after the honeymoon phase.

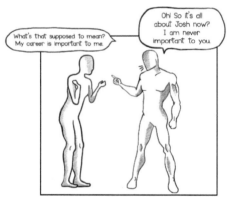

Mark - *"Sarah, I have booked this holiday for the both of us, we are leaving the day after tomorrow."*

Sarah - *"But Mark, I have a presentation due for Josh in 3 days, I am not sure how I will be able to go on a holiday. You should have asked me once."*

Mark - *"Oh! So, it's all about Josh now? I wonder why it's these men who always are a priority for you and never me."*

Sarah - *"What is that supposed to mean? My career is important to me."*

Consequences and implications:

The four stages of abuse within a toxic relationship can have severe consequences for the victim's well-being. In Sarah's case, the abuse took a toll on her self-esteem, emotional stability, and overall mental health. She constantly second-guessed herself. Over time, Sarah's sense of self-worth eroded, and she became isolated from friends and family due to the control exerted by Mark. The cycle of abuse, with its alternating stages, created a sense of dependency within Sarah, making it increasingly difficult for her to break free from the toxic relationship.

Recognizing the warning signs and seeking intervention at any stage of abuse is crucial for the well-being and safety of the victim. It was essential for Sarah to understand that the reconciliation and calm phases were temporary and designed to maintain control over her.

By understanding the four stages of abuse, their warning signs and the consequences, individuals can better recognize and address abusive dynamics. It is essential to prioritize the safety and well-being of victims by providing them with support, resources, and interventions to break free from the cycle of abuse and move towards a healthier future.

Abuse by Proxy

LINDA GREYMAN

Toxicity in relationships is a poison that can rot your heart and corrupt your life even by proxy.

The web of abuse can spread far and wide and you may find yourself trapped in a toxic person's web even when they are not directly involved in your life.

What is abuse by proxy?

Abuse by proxy is a form of emotional abuse where the abuser uses third parties to manipulate and control their victim. This can be friends, family, colleagues, or even institutions. The abuser will gather information, harass, and threaten the victim through these third parties and manipulate them to gain power over their target and discard them when they are no longer useful.

It's important to note that abusers lack empathy and only seek to gain control over their victim. In extreme cases, they may even harm people close to the victim, such as family members, friends, children or pets. To a toxic person, anything goes in the pursuit of power.

Abuse by proxy tactics

When a toxic person, especially a narcissist, can't control you directly they will use different tactics to spread their negativity and reign over you –

1. Flying monkeys

Remember the flying monkeys with feathered wings from The Wizard of Oz that the wicked witch used to terrorize others? A toxic person uses people in a similar way to abuse the victim. These flying monkeys are third parties who act on behalf of the abuser. They will stalk you, threaten you, manipulate you, tempt you with offers, spread lies about you - basically do anything the abuser asks them to without even realizing it. Anyone can be the abuser's flying monkey - family members, friends, children - anyone.

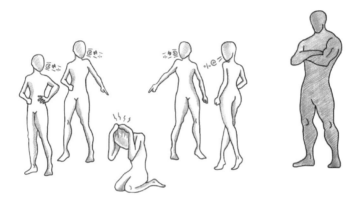

2. Smear Campaign

Smear campaigns are a well-thought-out plan to destroy you by spreading lies and false accusations about you. The abuser will fill the ears of others with rumors and gossip that discredit you and send them off to spread those poisonous lies which can damage your social reputation beyond repair. It also helps the abuser to hide their toxic nature as they are not directly involved in the entire campaign.

3. Triangulation

To make you more "submissive", the abuser will either introduce or use a third person in your relationship against you. The communication between all three of you will flow only through the abuser. Triangulation helps the abuser gain control by creating chaos between the involved parties, using misinformation, gaslighting and lies. The goal is to create confusion & doubt among two individuals so that the toxic person has the power in the relationship.

How abuse by proxy damages your life

The moment you start planning to leave your abuser, they will start planting the seeds of abuse by proxy. They will not think twice before employing family, friends, new partners, children, neighbors, and colleagues (both theirs and yours) to break you. Everyone is a pawn for the abuser, including authorities and institutions. They will build an army of enablers even before they have lost complete control over you.

The abuser will love-bomb, manipulate, intimidate and control everyone so that they can send their soldiers after you. They will pretend to be the victim and turn your own loved ones against you.

- They will spread ugly lies about you.
- Corrupt your children and turn them against you.
- Ruin your career by lying to your boss.
- File false reports with the authorities.
- Hurt or abduct your pet(s).
- Post false stories and your private photos on social media.

Nothing is off limits. They can and will do anything to destroy your social reputation. They will cripple your self-esteem and confidence. This is your punishment for not letting them control you. For standing up against them. For being finding the strength to leave them.

You will be stalked, threatened, coerced, and harassed. You will feel isolated, alone, afraid and unloved. You will fear for your loved ones' safety and will be forced to crumble under all the pressure, until you succumb and yield to your abuser.

Abuse by proxy can exist in any type of toxic relationship and will continue until the toxic person wins or finds a new target.

Rhett's Story

Dianne and Rhett dated for three years before breaking up. Although Rhett tried to save the relationship, Dianne was extremely critical of him and invalidated him at every opportunity. As Rhett tried to move on after their breakup and started dating again, Dianne constantly called and texted him and asked their friends to find out who he was dating.

Once she knew enough about Rhett's new partner Julia, Dianne immediately snooped on social media to find out some mutual friends that knew both Dianne and Julia. Being desperate, Dianne manipulated her friends to spread lies about Rhett being abusive and unfaithful. When Julia heard about the rumors, she became confused, alert and cautious. She decided to stay away from all the drama and refused to speak to Rhett further.

Although Rhett was the victim here, Dianne manipulated the whole situation to spread rumors about him by using her friends as flying monkeys and prevent Rhett from seeing anyone else, making him feel unsupported, rejected and lonely. Rhett felt powerless and like he had no control over the situation.

How to deal with abuse by proxy

1. Take steps to protect yourself and your loved ones - family, friends, children and pets.
2. Talk to people you trust. Remember, people who truly love you will never support someone who abuses you.
3. Reach out to your local abuse or domestic violence hotlines to seek help and find resources.

4. Seek therapy & join support groups to improve your mental health and self-esteem.

5. Keep records or a journal of the abuse to avoid self-doubts and the effects of gaslighting.

6. Talk to your employer about your situation so that your abuser has no access to your workplace.

7. Block the abuser and detach yourself from their enablers

8. Avoid reacting to lies and rumors about you.

9. Practice self-care - get enough sleep, avoid skipping meals, exercise, meditate etc.

If you find yourself trapped in abuse by proxy and think that you have been isolated with no one believing in you, then know that you can overcome this and heal yourself. Even when your family and friends have turned against you, don't doubt yourself for a moment. The truth will eventually take over.

Ambient Abuse

LINDA GREYMAN

Abuse is not always obvious, most of the time it is hidden and subtle and that's when it is most dangerous. Ambient abuse is when the abuser creates fear and confusion in the victim, making it easier to control them. Lost without any way to escape, the victim feels helpless and dependent on the abuser, giving the abuser total power and control.

What is ambient abuse?

Ambient abuse is a type of psychological abuse that creates a subtle but oppressive atmosphere of fear, unpredictability, and helplessness to manipulate and control the victim. Instead of abusing the victim directly, the abuser creates an intimidating atmosphere that manipulates the victim to submit to the toxic individual.

It is characterized by a pattern of behaviors, attitudes, and situations that erode a person's self-esteem, autonomy, and overall well-being over time. The abuser doesn't use physical violence, but instead, they manipulate the victim through intimidation, instability, anxiety, and constant tension. The effects of ambient abuse can be profound, as it slowly chips away at a person's sense of self-worth and leaves them feeling trapped, powerless, and emotionally drained.

The victim may doubt themselves, lack confidence and self-esteem, and feel powerless. They may feel isolated and confused as the abuser uses tactics like learned helplessness and gaslighting to control the victim, who may not even realize they are being abused.

Types of ambient abuse

Ambient abuse includes five categories that involve different behaviors aimed at creating an ambiance of intimidation and manipulation to control the victim –

1. Inducing disorientation

The abuser makes the victim feel confused and unsettled by using gaslighting, a manipulation strategy that makes the victim doubt themselves. The abuser will deny actions and behaviors repeatedly making the victim lose faith in their sense of reality, their abilities and their loved ones. As the line between reality and imagination is blurred by the abuser's constant lies, the victim becomes increasingly anxious of the unpredictability of their environment.

2. Incapacitating

The abuser makes the victim feel powerless and incompetent by withholding information, hiding items, refusing to help, and creating difficult situations where the victim has no option but to rely on the toxic person. The victim feels isolated and creates mental boundaries that make them more dependent on the abuser, who becomes indispensable and irreplaceable in the victim's life.

3. Shared psychosis (Folie à deux)

Folie à deux is when delusions and hallucinations are transferred from one person to another, often within a close family. So, when the abuser starts to assure the victim that both of them are going crazy, the victim starts to believe them. The abuser may convince the victim that they should stay away from others as everyone is trying to harm them. So, the victim becomes more isolated and refrains from talking about their abusive relationship to anyone.

The abuser will create imaginary threats and enemies and ask the victim to protect them. This makes the victim become more attached to and dependent on the abuser and becomes paranoid of others.

4. Abuse of information

The abuser is a prey that constantly stalks and monitors their target for gathering information. The better they know their victim, the better they can charm, control, manipulate and coerce their target for their own personal gain. Without hesitation, the abuser will misuse the victim's personal information irrespective of how unethically they have obtained them. Their only goal is to gain power and control over the victim.

5. Control by proxy

A type of abuse by proxy, the abuser recruits' others - family members, friends, neighbors, coworkers and others - to manipulate the victim. Instead of directly controlling the abused, the toxic person will manipulate loved ones - both theirs and the victim's - to do their dirty work. As the victim loses the support of family and friends, they become more isolated and reliant on the abuser.

Impact of ambient abuse

Manipulating a victim's environment can have severe long-term effects. This subtle form of abuse can make the victim appear crazy to others, causing loved ones to hesitate to believe or support them. Ambient abuse can also lead to serious mental health issues such as anxiety, depression, PTSD, and substance abuse.

Sadly, victims of ambient abuse often struggle to identify and escape the abuse. It's important to have faith in yourself and seek support from trusted loved ones.

Don't believe everything your abuser tells you and record all conversations and experiences as evidence. Make sure you, your children, your parents and other loved ones are safe and protected and find a safe place to escape to. Don't give in to your abuser's version of reality, trust yourself and know that healing is possible.

Connection between Toxic Relationship & Domestic Violence

Dr. KRISTIN DAVIN

When people think about domestic violence, they often think it's limited to physical assault or abuse towards a person. However, domestic violence extends well beyond the realm of physicality to include sexual, emotional, financial, or psychological abuse as well as physical aggression and controlling behaviors.

How domestic violence manifests in toxic relationships

A toxic relationship doesn't always start that way. It's often a subtle and gradual yet insidious growth of negative patterns that become toxic, which can lead to abuse. And once they become abusive, they are no longer just toxic, they are simply abusive. All your abuser wants is to control you.

It always starts small, subtle red flags that we ignore or miss out on entirely. And slowly it transforms, grows and evolves. And before you know it, toxic behaviors can quickly turn into repeated acts of abuse. Over time, you begin to feel worn down. Your self-esteem and self-worth plunge. The results are often long lasting and traumatic.

1. Red flags

It isn't uncommon for red flags to be ignored - especially in the beginning of a relationship. You are caught up in the excitement and newness of the relationship. You might be hesitant to bring anything up for fear of losing your partner because there are positive moments.

The excitement blinds you to some of the toxic behaviors. Maybe you justify their behaviors. Maybe you feel they are having a bad moment, a bad day. Something. You continue to kick the can down the road.

2. An unhealthy perspective

Because of an unhealthy perspective of relationships which often stems from your upbringing, attachment style, and previous relationships, you might believe that most relationships have ups and down and are prone to arguments and being verbally critical to one another.

You might also believe that if you continue to work hard enough and make changes, eventually your partner will change and the relationship will improve.

3. Blurred lines

Boundaries become blurred between the positive and negative interactions. You don't know if what is happening is healthy or unhealthy. You might find it is easy to ignore what your gut is telling you and put up with more negative behaviors.

If your partner is abusive or toxic and boundaries are not defined or set in the beginning of a relationship, it will be easy for them to overstep the boundaries, increasing their abuse and committing more horrible boundary violations.

A trauma bond

A trauma bond is a strong emotional bond developed with another person due to a recurring and cyclical pattern of abuse. These bonds are made even stronger by the intermittent reinforcement strategies used by the abuser through rewards and punishments.

Several long-term, negative consequences of trauma bonds include low self-esteem, a negative self-image and depression. The abuser will repeatedly and intentionally harm you through threat, intimidation, and manipulation – all with the goal of seeking power and control.

The irony is you continue to stay loyal to your partner who continues to violate you in horrific ways out of fear and mental and emotional distress and pain. Being in a trauma bond makes it merely impossible to walk away. But it is possible to change course and leave.

Carrie's Story

At the beginning of their relationship, Ryan pulled out all the stops and made Carrie feel alive. He gave her undivided attention. He was exciting to be around, full of energy, and intensity. But within a few months, Ryan became more emotionally and mentally abusive. She justified his behaviors as he was under a lot of stress at work. She worked harder not to upset him and took on a lot of the responsibility of the relationship.

But she never thought he would physically abuse her. But he did. And with one push it was the beginning. This would be followed by more physical abuse. Yet she stayed because after he would physically abuse her, it was always followed with promises not to do it again and great moments of love and care. Like it was in the beginning.

He justified his behaviors by telling Carrie that 'she made him do it' and that 'she instigated' his reactions. She could see some truth to that even though she knew he was being abusive. Her time and energy went towards pleasing him and doing what he wanted.

She started to doubt herself and became more depressed and anxious about doing things that may set him off. She turned inwards and her work suffered. She felt shameful for her situation so didn't talk to anyone about what she was going through. Eventually she gathered the courage to leave the relationship.

Without professional help or doing the work to identify the red flags early on, it is easy to remain stuck in an abusive and toxic relationship. The first step is always awareness and then finding ways to exit the relationship so that you can focus on yourself and have healthier relationships – not just with other people in your life, but most importantly with yourself.

Editor's Note

Are you suffering from domestic violence?

While signs of physical violence in intimate relationships such as repeated injuries, bruises or cigarette burns, may be easier to spot, indications of emotional intimate partner abuse can be really hard to notice.

Here's how to spot if someone is suffering from domestic violence:

- They strictly follow the instructions of their partner
- They are afraid of what their partner may think or say about their actions
- They lack confidence and independence
- They are constantly anxious, worried and uneasy
- They talk less than they used to
- They believe they are not good enough for their partner
- They are withdrawn and socially isolate themselves from friends and family
- They provide hints about their partner's violent and aggressive behavior

If you or someone you know is experiencing domestic violence, make sure to seek help immediately by talking to someone you trust, a therapist or the authorities.

Breaking the cycle of abuse and violence

Toxic behaviors can easily escalate into violent cycles of abuse as the abusive partner seeks to exert control and power over the victim, making it difficult for the victim to leave. Recognizing the signs of toxic behavior and seeking help can be crucial in breaking free from an abusive relationship and preventing further harm.

However, this can be challenging for victims as they feel isolated and dependent on their abuser. This is why it is essential to raise awareness of the signs of toxic relationships and domestic violence and to provide resources and support to victims. By breaking the cycle of abuse, we can promote healthy relationships built on respect, trust, and communication.

CHAPTER FIVE

BREAKING OUT OF THE TOXIC WEB

DEALING WITH TOXICITY

What Should You Do if You're in a Toxic Relationship?

LINDA GREYMAN

Being in a toxic relationship can be a distressing and overwhelming experience. It can have a significant negative impact on your physical, emotional and mental well-being. If you find yourself in a toxic relationship, it is essential to take steps to improve the situation and build a healthy relationship and life for yourself. This may involve seeking support from friends or family members, talking to a therapist, or ending the relationship altogether.

However, it's crucial to assess whether the toxic person is willing to change for the better. If they're not supportive, it's probably best to walk away and prioritize your own well-being. Every relationship is distinct, and it is vital to place self-care at the forefront and make choices that align with your personal growth and happiness.

Can a toxic relationship be healed?

Most people believe that toxic relationships cannot be "fixed" and that it is often better to simply walk away. But that's necessarily not the case. It depends on the intensity of toxicity in your relationship, the willingness of the toxic person to "change" and how badly it affects your mental and emotional well-being.

When both people involved are determined, dedicated and committed to make the relationship work by being supportive and sincere, an unhealthy relationship CAN become healthier. Toxic relationships can work when you stop trying to be competitive and rise above disrespect and criticism. For turning things around, the relationship must be mutually beneficial and evoke positive emotions in both individuals.

Working with a relationship counselor or a therapist can allow you to find a safe, unbiased space to openly talk about your issues without being judgmental. It can also help you to work through your challenges together and find new ways to resolve problems in the relationship.

However, if the toxic person is not willing to work with you to improve the relationship or if your reason for being in the abusive relationship is fear of loneliness, it is better to simply walk away. The only reason to stay in a toxic relationship and the only reason it can work is that both individuals genuinely care about each other despite their differences. If your relationship lacks love, then it's time to pack your bags.

213

How to "fix" a toxic relationship

If you aspire to transform your unhealthy relationship into a more positive and wholesome one, employing certain coping strategies can aid you on your journey. However, it's important to keep in mind that cultivating a healthy relationship requires ongoing effort and commitment from both partners, and a willingness to work together towards a better future.

1. Instead of being in denial, accept that you are in a toxic relationship. When you stop resisting your reality, your mindset will shift from fighting the toxicity to finding ways to cope with the stress and anxiety that come with a difficult relationship.

2. Have an honest heart-to-heart discussion with the toxic individual and clearly explain how their behavior and attitude is affecting you. The goal is to communicate your feelings, not complaining about them.

3. If talking to the toxic person proves futile, then talk to a trusted loved one or a therapist. Talking to someone else outside your primary relationship can help you gain a new perspective and better understand things.

4. Accepting your reality will help you take responsibility for your actions and understand what role you play in the toxic relationship. As they say, it takes two to tango.

5. As you learn to be more responsible in the relationship, stay away from the temptation to play the blame game. Focus on knowing and understanding one another better, instead of blaming each other.

6. Yes, the other person is toxic and manipulative, but unless they are abusive and dangerous (in which case you should leave immediately and seek help), you should try to have some empathy and compassion for them. Try to

understand why they behave the way they do and help them sort their issues.

7. A toxic relationship will eat away your self-esteem and confidence in no time. Boosting your self-esteem will empower you to better deal with your relationship issues and see yourself in a more positive light. Seeking therapy can help you learn healthier ways to resolve relationship issues.

When to move on from a toxic relationship

Once you have tried to "fix" your relationship and realize that the intensity of the negativity in the relationship is still too strong, then it may be time for you to leave the relationship.

When you are in a toxic relationship, you may feel shame and guilt when planning to walk away. Ending a relationship means accepting failure in something that has a lot of value to you. And failure is never easy to accept, especially when it involves your dreams and hopes. But staying in a toxic relationship past a certain point can be more damaging than walking away.

Unfortunately, not all relationships can be "fixed", especially the ones that are abusive. So, it's important to recognize when it's time to move on for the sake of your own well-being. If you find that the relationship is not healthy and is causing you more harm than good, it may be time to seek help and end the relationship.

Ending a relationship may become necessary when -

- You feel emotionally drained and constantly unhappy
- You don't feel safe

- Your partner doesn't share your values or support your goals
- You find it difficult to communicate with your partner
- Nothing seems to change no matter how hard you try
- Your partner doesn't meet your emotional or physical needs
- Your relationship lacks trust, honesty and sincerity
- You can't express yourself freely
- You can't afford to be your authentic self
- You feel trapped and suffocated

Ultimately, the decision to move on from a toxic relationship is a personal one and should be made based on your own feelings and experiences.

How to move on from a toxic relationship

Here are a few steps that can help you move on from a toxic, abusive relationship -

Step 1: Be assertive about your decision to leave. Tell yourself that the failure of the relationship is not your fault. Staying in the relationship will do you more harm than good until the toxic person actually puts in consistent effort to change

Step 2: Instead of leaving the relationship hastily, make a proper plan and chalk out the details like having a safe space to stay, having enough savings, access to all necessary documents etc. Plan ahead for everything and make sure to be as financially independent as you can before taking the big step.

Step 3: Seek support from loved ones. Walking away from a toxic relationship can leave you feeling depressed and relieved at the same time. Having the support of trusted loved ones will help you get through this difficult time. If needed, talk to a therapist about any issues that you may be facing.

Step 4: Go 'no contact' by cutting the toxic person off from your life and blocking them on social media. Do not communicate or interact with them unless absolutely necessary - such as for legal reasons or to co-parent. In case you have to interact, keep your responses brief and direct.

Step 5: Focus on healing your emotional wounds. Acknowledge your emotions and trust your intuition. Be patient with yourself and avoid negative self-talk that may result from months or years of abuse.

Step 6: Avoid having unrealistic expectations from your relationship and do not expect closure. The more you wait for closure, the harder it will be for you to heal. Let it go and remind yourself that it's okay to not get closure.

Here are some other things you can do to move on and heal from a toxic relationship –

- Set goals for personal growth.
- Address your needs and desires.
- Avoid unhealthy coping mechanisms like using alcohol & drugs.
- Forgive yourself and those who wronged you.
- Avoid blaming yourself for what happened.
- Pursue old hobbies or things you always wanted to do.
- Learn from your experience and grow.
- Save money and focus on your finances.

- Practice self-love and self-care.
- Live in the present moment, not the past or the future.

Do what your heart desires

Figuring out what you should do when you're in a toxic relationship and deciding to walk away will always be challenging. But the sooner you face the challenges, the healthier your relationship and your life will become.

The abuse and trauma you have experienced does not have to define your identity or your future. You are more than your abuse. You deserve a lot more. You deserve a future with a healthy relationship. And it can and will become a reality. You just need to take the right steps at the right time. Seek help and change your life.

How to Communicate with Toxic People in Relationships

KAYTEE GILLIS

Whether you have recently ended a relationship with a toxic partner and are attempting to be a parallel parent, or you have a toxic coworker or family member who you are unable to cut contact with, learning how to communicate with a high conflict or toxic person is essential to minimizing conflict.

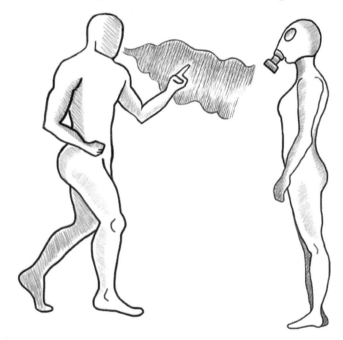

Tips to interact with a toxic person

Here are some tips that can help you communicate with a

toxic individual while maintaining healthy boundaries –

1. Pick your battles

Do not attempt to engage in every passive aggressive comment, snide remark, or rebuke every allegation and lie. Decide what is worth your time to focus on, and work on ways to ignore the rest. It is highly recommended that you keep a journal, even if it is on your phone.

When they try to engage with you, write a reply in your journal of the things you would like to say. This will help you see things in perspective.

2. Stick with minimal communication

If possible, going no contact is highly recommended, but that is not always possible or feasible, especially in cases with shared custody or if the person is a coworker or family member. However, here are a set of strategies that you can use when you have to engage with a toxic or abusive person in your life. This technique is called the "N.E.B. technique":

N for necessary

E for emotionless

B for brief

N: Ask yourself, "Is this communication or reply necessary?"

A nasty comment about your work ethic during the meeting? Ignore it. A text from your ex about requests for changes in childcare? This may warrant a reply. This helps you pick which communication is necessary to respond to.

E: Next, respond in an 'emotionless' way.

When you are communicating in an office meeting, be professional and concise with no emotion. When replying in an email or text, draft your reply in a word document, in order to avoid sending it before it is ready. It can be easy to fire off a response to someone who is being rude or passive aggressive, but this can just escalate the situation.

B: Lastly, make your reply or response 'brief'.

One or two sentences will usually suffice. If communicating through email or text, waiting a couple hours before replying is recommended, unless company policies or court orders state otherwise. This will allow you to reflect on your emotions and construct a professional and emotionless reply. If in person, take a breath, construct a reply in your head, and respond briefly.

Above all, it is imperative to conduct yourself professionally at all times. It is challenging not to react or to fight back, but it's essential to conduct yourself in a calm and respectful way, especially if communicating in front of others, such as children, mediators, or mutual coworkers.

Treat this person as you would someone who is insignificant to you: calm, firm, and no emotional reaction.

3.   Know your truth

This one is important because there will be times when you will doubt your own reality due to the gaslighting, triangulation, and other unhealthy communication that comes from many toxic people. It is common for someone who is toxic to claim the victim role, so be prepared to hear through others about all of the ways you have harmed them, or what a bad parent/friend/coworker/person you are, even if you know that these are lies.

Editor's Note

Communicating with toxic people in relationships can be challenging, but it is possible with the right strategies. Make sure to pick your battles, set boundaries, minimize contact, stay calm, and avoid getting drawn into their negative behavior.

Remember, you can only control how you respond to their behavior, not how the toxic person behaves. By using assertive communication, empathizing with their feelings, and seeking professional help, if needed, you can navigate toxic relationships in a healthier way.

How to Deal with Toxic Parents

KAYTEE GILLIS

As we become more comfortable talking about trauma and toxic relationships, it is important to include childhood trauma in this discussion.

Toxic parents and caregivers come in many forms. Some are emotionally avoidant; some are verbally or physically abusive. Some families teach children that their needs are not important, or perhaps send the message that the children are there to serve the caregivers. While not all toxic behaviors are necessarily abusive, having an understanding of the impact of toxic behaviors can help survivors move forward with healing.

A toxic childhood

When a child grows up in an environment that is dysfunctional, or even toxic, they do not realize that this is abnormal until adulthood, when they are able to look back on their experience with self-reflection and awareness. When it is the only thing they know, they do not yet realize that it is toxic.

People who grew up in toxic environments often continue these unhealthy patterns for many years unless they are able to receive support and develop self-awareness of their behavior patterns. Usually this comes after yet another failed relationship, or feelings of low self-esteem or poor self-worth that bring someone to a period of self-reflection.

"I do not want to engage in these patterns" is a common assertion from people who recognize that their experiences are contributing to negative feelings and experiences in

adulthood. It is often a lot harder to take the time to unlearn bad coping skills than to continue with what is already available to us. This is especially true if you are still living with your caregivers, or are struggling to break free of the hold their behaviors have over you.

Healing from growing up with toxic parents

These nine tips can help you in your journey toward healing and breaking the patterns of unhealthy behaviors that come from having toxic parents or caregivers:

1. Acknowledge the truth of your experiences

When children who grew up with toxic parents reflect on their history, it can bring up a lot of feelings of resentment, grief, and sadness. These feelings usually lead to unhealthy coping skills, or defense mechanisms such as denial or excusing the behavior.

Do not try to "justify" your experiences. Many people who grew up with emotional abuse or neglect are told that their experiences are "not as bad" as experiencing physical abuse. And still, those who grew up with physical abuse are often told that their experiences were justified for cultural, disciplinary, or other reasons. Do not let anyone tell you how you should feel about your experiences. Acknowledgement is the first step towards healing, and it can be done whether or not you have left the house yet.

You do not need to confront your parents or caregivers with your knowledge and experience to begin the healing process. Simply acknowledging that it was toxic and climbing out of denial is enough to start moving forward and healing.

2. Know what to expect, while understanding that you cannot change the past

While some adults do the work to heal and repair relationships that were harmed from their toxic behaviors, it is not realistic to expect parents to acknowledge their behaviors and the effects they had on you.

It is imperative to realize that you cannot go back and change it, and work on decreasing your expectations that they will have their "ah ha" moment and change. Many people feel let down by their experiences within the household due to expectations and hope that it could be better. Watching our friends with healthier families, or scenes on movies or social media remind us of what we do not have. But we are powerless to change this.

3. Find space for self-compassion every day

Children who grew up in toxic environments were either rarely shown compassion, or it was demonstrated in unhealthy ways. For example, they might have been shamed for asking for help or needing emotional or physical support. Furthermore, they were often shamed if they displayed signs of self-love or self-compassion. This is why it is crucial that you slowly make small changes to get used to showing yourself compassion, love, and understanding.

4. Increase the amount of self-care

Combat the stress experienced in your environment by making sure to take time to support your mental and physical health. Whether it is a solo journaling session, a hike with a friend, or a walk while listening to a podcast - preparing mentally and physically can help relieve the effects of interacting with any toxicity. Taking care of your body will help mitigate the stress you experience at home, and help support your mental health.

5. Work on creating healthy boundaries

Many people, especially people from enmeshed families or families with poor boundaries, struggle to even identify what their boundaries are. Start with thinking about what things make you uncomfortable or annoyed. For some, maybe it is not discussing certain topics such as politics or their love lives. For others, the boundaries might be around time spent together or activities done together.

When dealing with toxic families, having strong boundaries will help protect your mental health. Know what topics you will not participate in, such as conversations about dieting or relationships, so you can prepare to end the conversation if these topics arise. It is also important to know how long you are comfortable being present with those who display toxic behaviors. For some it is a few hours, others more or less.

When you start to feel uncomfortable, antsy, or argumentative, that is usually your internal cue to leave.

Be prepared for pushback, so have an excuse:

"I have to run an errand."

"A big project for work needs my attention."

6. Decrease opportunities to mirror their dysfunction

Living with people who are toxic can be very stressful. It is normal to find that you might even start engaging with your parents in the same dysfunctional ways they engage with you or each other. But try to limit this.

While it might feel good in the moment to argue back with them, and to tell them that their behaviors are frustrating or harmful, try not to engage with this. Doing so might actually make it worse for you if you have to live under their roof with nowhere to go. This might lead to an argument, with them refusing to let you win. If you match their dysfunction it can start to consume you.

7. Have an escape plan or an excuse to leave the house

If things start to get awkward or unsafe, have an "out" or a reason that you need to leave. This is especially important if you still live in their home and need to come up with a reason to leave. Whether it is needing to go to work, volunteering somewhere, going to the store, or visiting a friend- having an excuse to leave the situation can help protect your mental health from an uncomfortable environment.

If you are an adult and no longer financially dependent on your parents, use this as an opportunity to practice boundaries and leave their home if they act unsafe or their behaviors make you uncomfortable.

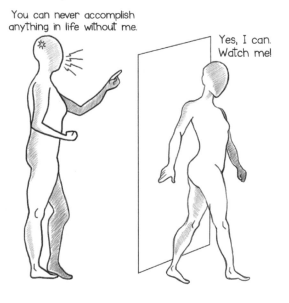

8. Be more open to learning and self-reflection on unhealthy patterns

When you are no longer living at home, it is important to look at your behaviors as opportunities for growth and exploration. It can be difficult to look at what we may be doing to contribute to unhealthy behavior patterns but being open to learning and self-reflection will help you grow.

Take a look at patterns of behaviors that repeat throughout your relationships, both platonic and romantic. Perhaps you find that you tend to shut down in relationships and want to change this. Or maybe you notice that you have been engaging in unhealthy coping skills such as substance use, overeating, or isolating.

These are not things that you will be able to change immediately but could be worked on along the journey of healing. It is easier to do this while no longer living at home, but it can be started at any time if you have the right support system.

9. Seek support

Social support can make all the difference during your healing process. Many people find they have the most support from their friends, social groups, colleagues, peers, or other people in their life. But support can also be from faith organizations, older people outside of the family such as aunts or uncles, grandparents, or people who do not participate in the toxic behaviors.

Seek people who make you feel understood and valued, and this will make all the difference in your healing. You may also seek help from a therapist or a mental health professional as well.

10. Find ways to heal and find meaning

Many people have used their experience to find meaning and purpose. Some use their knowledge and healing to help others, while others find support in their journey of personal growth. Support groups, journaling, and therapy can help you get there.

Editor's Note

Finding meaning can help you create new narratives that can add a sense of purpose and coherence to all the toxicity you have experienced since your childhood. Healing and finding new meaning in life can help to improve your mental and emotional well-being and make you feel more closely connected to yourself.

How to Deal with a Toxic Partner

Dr. KRISTIN DAVIN

Couples develop a unique "dance" with each other that becomes a habitual pattern over time. In healthy relationships, this dance is positive and reinforces each partner's well-being. However, toxic relationships create a negative and painful dance that slowly burns away at the couple's happiness.

A toxic dance mindset

The toxic dance mindset consists of a foundation built on name-calling, keeping score, and a "tit for tat" attitude. Partners criticize, show contempt, and defend themselves against each other. They develop a disdain for one another, and resentment becomes a pervasive feeling in the relationship. It's always "me vs you" and never just "us".

A crucial aspect of a toxic relationship is a lack of empathy, where partners are unable to understand or empathize with each other. They don't feel heard, seen, or validated, and their feelings are disregarded.

This creates feelings of unimportance, depletion, overwhelm, frustration, and feeling stuck.

The mistrust that exists between partners further erodes the relationship, leading to chronic arguments that never get resolved. This type of interaction undermines trust, safety, and security, making it challenging to change the pattern of toxicity.

The cracks in the foundation leaves each person emotionally and mentally exhausted. Each day renders feeling more hopeless and helpless to make any sustainable, positive changes. They are fearful about how long they can live this way and wonder if they will ever get out of this pattern of toxicity.

Strategies for living with a toxic partner

When you find yourself in a situation where leaving a toxic relationship is not an immediate option, it's essential to have tools and strategies to help you manage it differently.

Here are five strategies that can help you cope with a toxic partner and decide how to build a healthier future for yourself.

1.   Set healthy boundaries

Knowing where to draw the line is crucial for your emotional and mental health. Initially when you start to set boundaries, it is not uncommon to feel guilty or for the person to try and make you feel guilty for changing your ways because you are putting your needs first. And it is equally not uncommon for the other person to give you push back as they will not like this. But that's ok.

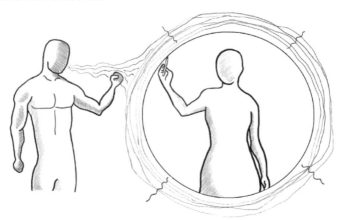

Boundaries include how much time you will spend with them and what that time might look like. This may be more difficult if it is a current partner or an ex-spouse, but doing what you can to limit your time with them is also part of setting healthy boundaries.

For example –

- Less communication
- Less back & forth
- Having a plan of what will and will not be discussed

Learning how to maintain clear boundaries and limits around toxic behavior is one of the first steps to healing and moving away from their toxic behavior.

2. Ignore their drama.

Most people who are toxic, are dramatic. They gossip, criticize, complain, play the victim, and manipulate. They want to bring you into their drama and be part of their conversation. They don't take responsibility for their actions and twist things making you feel like you are in the wrong.

They will point the finger at another person. They will challenge you when you try to set boundaries to continue the same relational dance. Their drama leaves you exhausted. So simply avoid their drama and pay no attention to their manipulative mind games.

3. Communicate with them

Although this can be one of the more challenging things to do, talking to them about how their toxic behavior is making you feel or how it is harming you, might help them gain a new perspective and provide a different conversation to take place.

For example, the person may not be aware that they are being toxic – so pointing this out to them might be helpful. Come from a place of calm, be less emotionally charged and stick to the topic.

4. Don't try to fix things or them

It's not uncommon, especially for women, to want to jump in and fix things. If you are conflict avoidant, you might want to fix the situation or the other person instead of addressing their underlying toxic behavior. However, unless they want to change, you will be left feeling more exhausted and frustrated.

Maybe you have tried this to no avail. Learning how to own what is yours and discard the rest, helps you stay focused on self.

5. Speak to a professional

Often speaking to a mental health professional or a therapist who has experience helping others with toxic relationships can help you take small steps to making change – on your end. Doing this will help you feel more in control and empowered in your life. A professional can provide the tools that you need to manage this challenging relationship.

If you find that you are unable to completely leave this relationship because of your circumstances – a partner you are married to and have to stay with due to financial or medical reasons or an ex-partner you co-parent with - it would be beneficial to find ways to cope and co-exist with this toxic person without affecting your emotional and mental health.

However, there are situations that no matter how much you do to set healthy boundaries, ignore the drama, or communicate your concerns, you realize it is too toxic to stay. Ask yourself –

"Have I done everything I think I can to address the toxic behavior?"

If yes, *"Have they done anything to change on their part?"*

"How will ending this relationship or quitting this job change things for me?"

Asking and answering those questions are key to coming up with a plan that is best for you and your well-being.

How to Deal with Toxic Relatives and Friends

Dr. Josh Gressel

As we delve into the complexities of toxic relationships, we will deal with the ones that are most intertwined with our lives- close family members and relatives. These bonds are forged in blood, making it difficult to escape interactions with them. Furthermore, dealing with their toxicity can be much more challenging than with distant relatives. However, as we discuss the dynamics of such relationships, we will also draw parallels with friendships, as many of the same principles apply regardless of the degree of separation.

Dealing with toxic relatives

Toxic family members can be challenging to deal with, because whether you want to or not, you love them. You can be angry and hurt and you keep saying "I'm done with them!" repeatedly. But even if you do cut them off, it's unlikely that you can cut them off internally. They will still occupy an outsized amount of mental real estate.

The second major challenge with toxic family members is that they really don't bring out the best in you. Depending on where you fit in the family dynamic, just being in their presence will likely cause a regression in you to the way you were when you grew up with them. So, you will have less of your adult self-available to contend with them when you feel the poison of their toxins. Despite your best intentions, you are likely to be more of a child than an adult in how you respond to their toxicity.

The best any of us can do in dealing with toxic close relatives is to be as conscious as we can be of the many feelings, we have in our relationship with them. If it was just the toxic piece, the answer would be far easier. But we also love them, care about them, want their approval and love, and worry about them as these feelings come naturally with growing up with them.

So do your best to integrate all you feel for them and be forgiving of yourself for feeling confused or uncertain with how to handle them. You may think you're failing because you can't find the right answer for how to be with them. But you are actually being the best possible version of yourself.

Dealing with toxic friends & distant relatives

If they're so toxic, is it right for you to be with them? Are they toxic with everyone, or just you? In other words, is it who they are, or what your relationship has become that is the problem? There is a kind of decision tree to be navigated before you can find the best answer on what to do.

In most cases, the reason your friends with someone who's toxic is that initially they weren't toxic. It's something that either developed over time or that you woke up to over time. This brings you to the next fork in the decision tree:

Are they toxic with most people, or just with you?

If it's the former, then you need to think about why you would want to stay involved with someone you have discovered is toxic.

How is this serving you?

In most cases, with enough awareness, you will realize that the cons far outweigh the pros, and you are best to work your way out of this person's life.

But if you have reason to know that they are really toxic only with you, then the issue lies in your relationship, not in the person. In that case it's worth exploring with this friend what the heck is going on.

Do they see you as toxic? Is there something to be done to fix this relationship? You won't know the answer to this question until you address it with the person involved.

In either instance, the answer is not to directly declare the person as toxic. It is to look at the layers of truth in the relationship and to do your best to integrate them all before responding.

Editor's Note

Tips to deal with toxic relatives & friends

If you are stuck with toxic close relatives or friends, here's how to make things better and more positive –

1.   Be prepared for their toxicity

Be mentally prepared before you meet or interact with them so that you can protect yourself.

2.   Avoid arguing with them

Don't fall victim to their provocation. While it may be hard to hold back your reactions, avoid arguing with them.

3.   Keep things private

Don't share your personal information with them, especially about your career and romantic relationships.

4.   Avoid trying to fix them

A toxic person can never change without self-awareness and therapy. So do not waste your time expecting them to change no matter how hard you try.

5. Practice forgiveness

Learn to forgive them instead of holding on to grudges. However, forgiveness does not mean forgetting the past.

Once you have tried all possible ways to handle things sensibly and maturely and if the situation still remains the same, it may be best to leave the relationship without any remorse, guilt or shame.

6. Limit your contact

Go no contact with them without feeling guilty about protecting yourself. If no contact is not possible, limit your interactions with them.

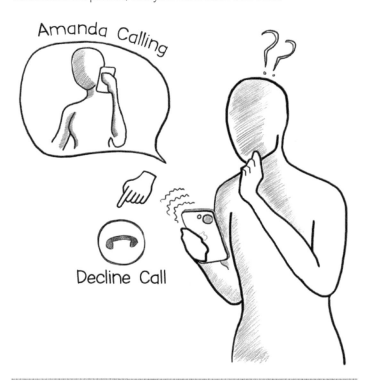

How to Deal with a
Toxic Boss / Coworkers

LINDA GREYMAN

The impact of a boss or manager on your work experience cannot be overstated. A supportive boss can advance your career and provide opportunities, while a toxic one can make each workday unbearable.

Working in a toxic environment can seriously affect your performance, productivity and motivation in the workplace and lead to stress, anxiety, burnout and depression.

If you're dealing with a toxic boss, it's important to maintain your well-being while navigating the situation.

How to deal with a toxic boss

If you think you have a toxic, narcissistic boss, then here's how you can start to make things better at the workplace –

1. Understand what they expect from you

To overcome confusion about expectations, schedule a conversation with them to ask for clarity. Inquire about their priorities, challenges, and communication preferences. Try to find out what the root of the issue is, provide feedback without emotion and always seek clarity about projects, instructions and your conduct.

If that's not possible, observe their interactions with others to gain insight. Once you understand their expectations, assess how well you're meeting them and work on improving where necessary.

2. Don't take it personally

Don't take everything personally and let go of your ego. Remember that their behavior is not necessarily a reflection of your performance. If your boss consistently exhibits condescending, overly critical, or insecure behavior, it's likely they act this way with others as well. Seek feedback from coworkers and others to gain perspective. Control what you can - your thoughts, feelings and reactions. Stay focused on your career goals and stick to your personal values.

3. Be empathetic

Understand why your boss behaves in a toxic way. Pause and take a step back to analyze the behaviors of your boss which often arises out of past trauma, insecurities, chronic stress, personality disorders etc.

4. Focus on your work

Instead of focusing on your feelings, focus on doing a better job. Be more efficient, make fewer mistakes, and be more productive. As you become more skilled and proficient in your job, your focus will shift towards growing and succeeding instead of unnecessary office politics. It's also important that you avoid seeing yourself solely as a victim and instead focus on developing professional skills.

5. Document everything

Ask for written instructions and briefs, communicate over email, use statistics and data to back your actions, and document all interactions you have with your boss in your personal device. If needed, you can inform HR or your boss' boss.

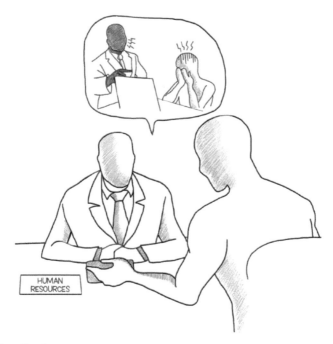

6. Seek support

Create a supportive network at work with people who can offer guidance, support, and feedback. They can be team members, mentors or sponsors. Building these relationships can pay off in the long run, especially with senior leaders who can increase your visibility and create new opportunities for you.

7. Build your confidence

Toxic workplaces can erode your confidence, so protect it by creating a fulfilling life outside of work. Try new hobbies, spend time with loved ones, or do something relaxing after work. Separating your identity from your career is essential for maintaining your peace of mind and self-worth.

8. Decide to stay or leave

If you feel drained and suffocated, decide if leaving your job will be a better option for your mental health. However, as this decision can have some serious consequences on your life, make sure to think it through.

How to deal with toxic coworkers

Dealing with a toxic coworker can be a nightmare and it can affect your motivation, performance and job satisfaction. Here are some steps to protect yourself –

1. Learn, understand, communicate

Observe the thought and behavior patterns of your toxic colleagues. Be empathetic and try to understand what is going on with them. When you understand their drives and motives, have an honest conversation with them about how their behavior affects you without judging or accusing them. No matter how they respond, you will have a better plan of action moving forward.

2. Control your emotions & reactions

Make sure to manage your emotions, energy and how you react to the toxic person. Control what you can, which is yourself and try to de-escalate the situation professionally and tactfully. Be more mindful about your thoughts and emotions to cut the drama out. Do not allow your emotions to take over.

3. Establish boundaries

Be strict about your personal boundaries and keep things completely professional. Interact with your toxic coworker only when it is absolutely necessary and keep communication limited to work related issues. Avoid gossiping about them and carry yourself with dignity. Keep your interactions strictly limited and avoid them like the plague.

4. Talk to your boss

When all else fails, it may be best to talk to your superiors about the toxic coworkers' behavioral issues. You can ask your HR or your manager to establish stricter rules of conduct within teams to eradicate negative & toxic practices.

Don't allow toxicity to affect your career

Toxicity in the workplace can suck all the positivity out of you. It can not only affect your emotional and mental well-being, but your career as well. However, when you use healthy coping mechanisms to deal with such toxicity, it can steer you towards the right direction, protect your mental health and drive your career forward.

Dealing with Aggressive Behavior in Toxic Relationships

LINDA GREYMAN

When you are in a toxic relationship, dealing with hostility, confrontation and aggression can become extremely exhaustive and draining. Toxic individuals thrive in drama, noise and chaos. Regardless of how much you may want to avoid unwanted confrontations and aggressive behavior, it will rear its ugly head quite often and make things more complicated.

For the sake of clarity, aggression is any behavior, whether verbal or non-verbal, that involves attacking another person with the intention of harming them.

How to deal with aggressive behavior

If you have to interact with a toxic, aggressive individual on a regular basis, whether in your personal life or otherwise, here are a few steps to deal with them and lessen the tension-

Step 1: Make sure to keep yourself and others safe

When facing a toxic person with aggressive behavior patterns, the first thing you should do is make sure you and your loved ones are safe. A hostile person can become unpredictable during a confrontation, so it is crucial that you protect yourself, and your family members or team members if you are at work. If it becomes extremely intense, walk away from the situation. Contact the authorities and take legal action if needed.

However, not all toxic people necessarily become physically violent or dangerous even when they become aggressive and, in most cases, you can deal with them by yourself. While there is no specific general approach, you can safely and effectively protect yourself from the aggressor with certain strategies discussed below. But it is best to have emergency numbers at hand and be prepared to seek help if the situation gets out of your hand.

Step 2: Remain calm and do not panic or retaliate

While it may be tempting to retaliate or argue back and give them a piece of your mind, choose to keep your cool and refrain from escalating the situation. Instead of reacting negatively, which may come naturally, focus on controlling your emotions and approach the situation calmly. You can say something like −

"I understand you are angry and your feelings are hurt, but let us try to calm down and have a mature discussion. I am sure there is a way to solve this."

If nothing seems to calm them down, simply take a few deep breaths and ignore them. No matter how much they shout or swear, remain silent, undisturbed and calm. Do not try to confront them or take their words personally. Being calm will also allow you to detach from the situation and analyze what's going on more closely to make smarter decisions. Avoid trying to solve their issues, but show kindness and concern.

Step 3: Listen, understand and be empathetic

Yes, you should do exactly what you don't want to do right now - listen to what the toxic, aggressive person has to say. While their words may turn into screams, they are still trying to express their emotions, albeit in an unhealthy manner. Listening to the aggressive person can often make them calmer as regardless of how stubborn or aggressive they may appear, they simply want to get your attention, be heard, reassured and validated.

When you remain calm in an aggressive confrontation, you will be better able to understand what the toxic person is trying to say, understand what the underlying issue is and address it compassionately.

While it may be difficult to be kind when the other person is screaming at you, try to show some empathy and vulnerability as it can help the toxic person calm down. Your focus should be on de-escalating the situation, not aggravating it further.

Step 4: Set firm and non-negotiable boundaries
Boundaries will help to define what is acceptable for you and will protect you from threats and harm. Setting boundaries and communicating them clearly without feeling guilty is crucial for drawing the line. Whenever the toxic person tries to violate your boundaries with aggression, you can simply leave the room or stop engaging with them.

Make sure to stay firm about your boundaries and do not hesitate to enforce them. To establish your boundaries, you may say —

"I will not listen to a single word you say unless you calm down and talk to me respectfully."

Step 5: Dodge the drama and learn to say 'no'
Toxic people need drama and chaos to survive. They can create drama out of even the most mundane things like washing the dishes. They will use manipulation, aggression and emotional abuse tactics to pull you into their drama so that they can feel better by degrading you. The best way to deal with dramatic and aggressive behavior is to avoid getting involved in the chaos.

Instead of getting drawn into it, whether out of concern or curiosity, learn to say "no". Be firm and assertive about removing yourself from the drama even when they threaten you with a dramatic outburst. In case the toxic person has become extremely verbally aggressive, choose to remain silent and avoid giving them any attention. When you refuse to speak and avoid sharing your opinions, you get to control the situation.

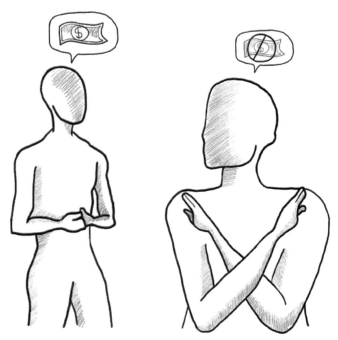

Step 6: Be strategic in your approach and stay detached

When you realize that a toxic person has the tendency to become aggressive, then you need to strategize your moves accordingly by getting detached from the situation. Here are some additional steps you can take to get the situation in your control -

- Do not minimize their emotions
- Have an open line of communication
- Maintain non-threatening eye contact while communicating
- Understand when to remain silent and when to respond appropriately
- Maintain a safe distance from the aggressor
- Talk to them about their aggressive behavior
- Avoid telling them to "calm down" or demanding specific behavior
- Do not assume things
- Know how to deal with threats and avoid giving threats or ultimatums
- Resist the urge to try to "fix" them
- Encourage them to seek professional help

Step 7: Realize that it is NOT your fault and you don't deserve to be abused

Toxic people often react aggressively due to their own inability to regulate their emotional reactions. It has nothing to do with anything you said or did. While the toxic person may behave aggressively or in a passive-aggressive way to make you feel guilty, do not rationalize abuse, blame yourself or lose faith in yourself. The most important step you can take in dealing with toxic aggression is realizing that you do not deserve abuse.

Stay calm to stay in control

When dealing with aggressive behavior in a toxic relationship, the most important and helpful strategy is to remain calm and composed. React less, listen more. Understand their issues and show empathy, but do not try to fix them. The more you control your own emotions, the better you will be able to deal with them.

In case you feel reactive, pause and take a deep breath before acting out as it can make the situation much worse. Self-control is the key to gaining control over an aggressive person. If you are worried about your or your loved ones' safety, then make sure to seek help immediately. You can reach out to local authorities, support organizations, emergency services, or get a restraining order, or talk to a trusted friend or family member.

Is it Possible to Fix a Toxic Relationship?

DR. ANGEL J. STORM

Relationships are not 50/50. They are 100/100. It requires committed effort from both partners, not just half-hearted attempts to "fix" things. Before attempting to fix a toxic relationship, it's important to first understand its dynamics. Consider asking yourself the following questions as a starting point for gaining that understanding:

Is my partner available to me?

Is my partner reliable?

Do I have to walk on eggshells around my partner?

Can I express myself openly to my partner?

Do I feel like I'm not good enough for my partner?

Am I the one who must apologize in order for our relationship to work?

Has my partner ever cheated on, threatened, or controlled me?

What actions has my partner done in the past 90 days to make me believe this relationship is a priority to him/her?

Is it love? Probably not!

Identifying a toxic relationship can be difficult, particularly because your perspective may differ from your abuser's. While your abuser may have said all the right things and even appeared to make efforts to benefit the relationship, it's essential to examine their underlying motivations. Failure to do so can result in further gaslighting and continued abuse.

Refusing to acknowledge a relationship as toxic in the name

of love won't solve the problem or transform it into a healthy one. Both partners must be willing to contribute 100% to nurture and strengthen the bond. If one partner is unwilling or uninterested in doing so, the relationship cannot improve.

Consider your love language. If it's receiving gifts, but your partner only buys you gifts once or twice a year, is this respectful of you and your connection? Is the relationship built solely on your partner's terms? These questions can help you understand whether your relationship is truly founded on love or something else entirely.

Know your reality

Having a realistic perspective on the relationship is critical in order to determine where to put your time, energy and money. If your partner is unwilling to fulfill your needs for love, validation, and security, you must acknowledge this truth within yourself first.

The next step to consider before determining if you can fix a toxic relationship is your partner's perspective. You and your partner must be at the same starting point in order to move forward together in unison. You must both be looking at the same picture and be willing to work towards the same goal.

If your partner is refusing to see how damaging their words and actions are to you and the relationship, there is no fixing that connection, no matter how long you put it off, what words you use to describe the relationship or how hard you try to make it work.

So, if you're questioning whether or not your relationship is toxic, ask yourself this: *"Am I willing to call the relationship what it is?"*

If you can't label it, you can never hope to fix it. But if you and your partner are both able and willing to confront the toxicity head-on, there's a chance that - through determination and baby steps - you could someday rebuild what was broken.

How to Fix
a Toxic Relationship

LINDA GREYMAN

Healing a toxic relationship is possible when both individuals are willing to put in the effort and commitment to build a better future. Once you acknowledge the fact that you are in a toxic relationship, you can work with the other person towards overcoming the toxicity and building a healthier, happier relationship.

Steps to heal a toxic relationship

Step-1: Realize that the relationship has become unhealthy and toxic. Denial will only prolong the problems.

Step-2: Communicate in an open, honest and non-judgmental way, instead of being rude. Practice active listening and empathy. Avoid blaming, name-calling, and sarcasm.

Step-3: Establish clear boundaries and openly communicate behaviors that bother you and need to change. Set clear limits and expectations.

Step-4: Address underlying deeper issues that lead to toxicity like lack of trust, resentment, insecurity, control, and anger. Work through these issues together.

Step-5: Limit conflict triggers, avoid hot-button issues, minimize disagreements, and de-escalate arguments when they arise. Let go of past grudges and start fresh, as holding onto the past can lead to toxicity.

Step-6: Recognize how your behavior is contributing to the problem. Are you enabling the toxic person by making excuses for their behavior?

Step-7: Instead of keeping score, be more accountable for your own actions and apologize for your mistakes.

Step-8: Consult a therapist and consider couple's counseling as it can help you and your partner deal with toxic and abusive behaviors. Talk to trusted loved ones as they can help you gain a new perspective about the situation.

Step-9: Practice self-care and focus on healing yourself by addressing your unmet needs, acknowledging your emotions and taking time for yourself.

Step-10: Take a break and spend some time apart if needed. It can help provide perspective and the motivation to improve the relationship when you come back together.

Step-11: Practice empathy and compassion for yourself and for the toxic person, even if you don't agree with their actions.

Step-12: Be patient and give each other the space needed to transform, improve, and mature.

Step-13: Validate each other's feelings by making an effort to understand each other's perspectives and emotional needs, without judgment.

Step-14: Make time for fun activities together. Appreciate each other and express gratitude to rebuild intimacy and closeness.

Step-15: Trust your instincts as it can help you to make decisions that prioritize your well-being.

Be willing to leave the relationship if things don't work. Don't be desperate. Be detached instead. While it can be difficult to let go of a relationship, sometimes it's necessary for your own well-being. It's important to recognize that you deserve to be in a healthy and fulfilling relationship, and if the toxic behavior continues, it may be time to consider ending the relationship.

Your relationship won't heal unless you heal yourself

Change can occur only when both parties involved are equally willing and interested in changing the toxic relationship dynamic. Working with a professional can help you learn healthy coping mechanisms to move forward towards a healthier and more positive future.

While the journey can be extremely challenging, in the end it can be worth it. Change is difficult, but it is possible.

How to Leave
a Toxic Relationship

DOMINIQUE INKROTT &
FORREST TALLEY

Ending a relationship can be difficult to execute for many people, and the process can be even more difficult when you are ending a toxic relationship. The process of ending a relationship starts with accepting the reality that the relationship is not working and needs to end. In the case of an unhealthy relationship, of course, the reality is that the relationship is toxic.

Unfortunately, toxic relationships do not tend to resolve themselves or improve organically. When you finally take the initiative to end the relationship for your own wellbeing.

Steps to ending a toxic relationship

Ending a toxic relationship is a process that can be broken down into the following steps -

1.   Formulate an exit plan for leaving the relationship

In many cases, this means deciding when and where you will have the "breakup conversation" with your partner, and identifying what you want to say. It often helps to give yourself some practice by rehearsing this conversation out loud - whether you are saying the words to yourself, to your dog, or to a trusted friend.

2.   Make safety your top priority

Sometimes a relationship may be so toxic or volatile that there are safety concerns. Do whatever is needed to stay safe both during and after the breakup. When leaving any toxic relationship - whether or not there are safety concerns - the most important thing is leaving.

It is great to have the catharsis of a thoughtful breakup conversation, but at the end of the day, what matters is leaving the relationship and maintaining your safety and wellbeing.

3. Be deliberate and seize the opportunity to end the relationship

Toxic relationships do not end themselves. An "ideal" time and place to break up will never materialize - the ideal time to end the relationship is as soon as possible once you realize that the relationship is toxic beyond repair. In some cases, you may reach a point when you are confronted by your partner's toxic behavior and become so upset in the moment that you are driven to end the relationship on the spot.

If the moment for a breakup presents itself, you should certainly take it, but these spontaneous breakups are lucky and rare. Whether spontaneous or planned in advance, it is up to you to create the opportune moment, no matter how inconvenient or awkward it may feel.

4. Make a clean break after leaving

It can be tempting to stay in contact with your ex, especially if they are reaching out expressing sadness, trying to make you feel guilty for leaving, or attempting to win you back. Toxic partners will often use manipulative tactics to exploit your emotions and lure you back into the relationship.

As much as you may want to respond, you can save yourself a lot of heartache by maintaining a "no-contact" policy. The best thing you can do after the breakup is to sever all ties. Don't try to stay friends, don't respond if he/she calls or texts, and don't reach out when you're feeling lonely.

It may take significant willpower initially, but with time and consistency, maintaining a "no contact" policy will become natural. Moreover, a clean break makes it easier for you to move on with your life and enjoy healthier relationships in the future.

5. Be deliberate in moving forward from the relationship

The end of a relationship - even a toxic one - can leave you feeling lonely and sensing a void in your life where that relationship used to take up significant time and energy. This can lead to poor decisions like getting back together with your ex or rushing into another relationship. You must guard yourself against this. Fill the "void" left by the relationship by committing your time to productive and meaningful pursuits.

Invest in your other relationships by spending time with your family and friends and getting involved with a church or volunteer group in your community. Devote your extra time to working on projects that you are passionate about and have not yet had time to commit to, or developing new hobbies or skills that you find engaging or rewarding.

Not only does it help you to move forward, but it also helps you to become a better version of yourself and prepares you for healthier relationships in the future.

Helping a Toxic Person

LINDA GREYMAN

Being in a relationship with a toxic person can take a significant toll on your emotional and mental wellbeing, leading to feelings of bitterness, resentment, and indifference. However, it's essential to tap into your innate empathy and find the strength to rise above the negativity to help the toxic person heal.

By supporting them in addressing their internal issues, such as past trauma, and facilitating their healing journey, you can bring a positive transformation to your relationship. Over time, as the toxic person begins to heal, their negative patterns of behavior may gradually fade away, creating a more positive, healthier relationship between the two of you.

Understanding is the first step to helping

Why should you even care about helping someone who abuses you?

It's common to question why you should extend help to someone who has caused you harm and engaged in abusive behavior towards you. But the honest truth is you are not like the toxic person in your life. And you have the ability to show empathy, compassion, kindness, care and love.

The first step to helping someone who has been abusive towards you is to try and understand why they behave the way they do. It's essential to understand that toxic behavior often stems from a range of underlying factors, such as unresolved past trauma, unmet needs and desires, an intense need for love, admiration, attention, and validation, insecurities and fears, dissatisfaction, childhood abuse, and underlying psychological conditions like narcissism and borderline personality disorder.

By learning more about what drives a person to behave in a toxic manner, you can gain a better understanding of the situation and take steps to heal the individual and your relationship. This understanding can also help you gain control over the situation, promoting a healthier dynamic between you and the toxic person.

How to help a toxic person heal

Here are a few steps and strategies that will enable you to help a toxic person heal and make your relationship with them better –

1.   Know if they are willing to change

You can't help a toxic person who's unwilling to change. This can be a serious problem as people with toxic personalities often do not realize there is something "wrong" with them. However, certain circumstances can make them realize their behavior is hurting loved ones, making them more open to healing. Only then can you start helping them.

2.   Encourage them to seek professional help

Toxicity is generally born out of early life trauma, personality disorders, mental health issues and other underlying internal conflicts. Therapy can help a toxic person understand and cope with their inner struggles, modify their behavior, improve empathy, and enhance relationships. Research has shown that therapy can promote adaptive patterns of thinking, feeling, and acting, as well as a sense of autonomy and agency in individuals with narcissistic personality disorder.

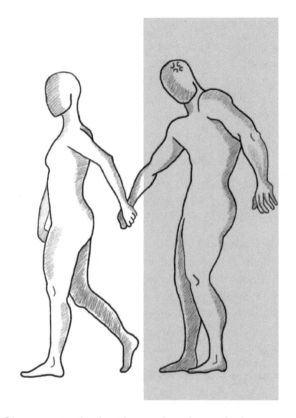

3. Show empathy but have clear boundaries

Being kind, empathetic, and compassionate to someone who abuses you is difficult but important to help them heal. Acknowledge their emotions, reassure them, and show affection while maintaining firm personal boundaries. Communicate boundaries clearly and calmly reject toxic behavior. When they mistreat you, you can say -

"I understand how you feel and I realize how I could have done it differently to avoid offending you, but such aggressive behavior is not acceptable for me."

4.   Accept them as they are

Acceptance is a crucial step in supporting a toxic person, particularly if you have a close relationship with them. When attempting to help a toxic person, it's important to clarify your intention and remain focused on your goal of helping them heal and cope with their inner issues. It's essential to let go of any expectations of how they should behave and instead concentrate on genuinely aiding them in living a better life. While you may not necessarily like them for who they are, it's important to understand that if they could change themselves; they would have done so already.

5.   Practice self-love

Helping a toxic person heal can be draining, so it's important to prioritize self-care. Address your own needs, love yourself, and have a support system to share your feelings. Consider talking to a therapist about your own mental and emotional health

A toxic person can 'change'

It's important to remember that a toxic person can change and develop healthier patterns of thought and behavior, but ultimately, it's not your responsibility to fix them. While you can support them in their journey, it's crucial to prioritize your own well-being and the safety of your loved ones who are not abusive. So, do your best to help, but know when to step back and prioritize your own needs.

Helping and Supporting a Loved One in a Toxic Relationship

LINDA GREYMAN

People in toxic relationships often find it difficult to talk about the abuse they experience. Hence, they keep their suffering to themselves and refrain from seeking help and support. This is why it is important that we reach out to our friends and loved ones to support them when we suspect they are trapped in a toxic relationship.

How to help someone in a toxic relationship

When attempting to assist a loved one who is stuck in a toxic relationship, it is important to approach the situation with sensitivity and consideration. Here are some suggestions for respectfully reaching out and providing support to your loved one –

1.   Talk to them

Have an open conversation with your loved one and share your concerns with them. Gently tell them that you are worried about them. For instance, you may ask –

"Hey, how have you been? You seem different. Is there anything you want to talk about? You can trust me with whatever you are going through. I am all ears."

If your friend feels comfortable enough, they may start opening up to you and share their issues. But it is crucial that you listen to them without judgment or criticism.

2. Do not ask your friend to leave the relationship

While it may make all the sense in the world to leave an abusive relationship, it is easier said than done. Often the victim is severely manipulated by the abuser and they lose their ability to make decisions on their own. So, avoid being overly practical and don't force your loved one to simply "walk away".

3. Reassure them and validate their emotions

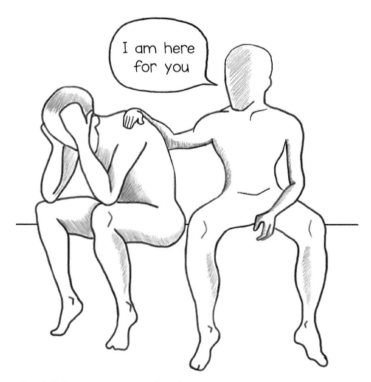

Gaslighting is an emotional manipulation tactic that can make the victim constantly doubt themselves. By providing validation to your loved one, you can reassure their emotional experience. This can help them gain confidence in themselves.

4. Spend more time with them

Toxic people usually isolate their victims and prevent them from interacting with others. Staying in contact with the victim through emails, phone calls, texts, social media or by visiting them in person can help them overcome loneliness and isolation.

5. Build their self-esteem

You can help them to rebuild their sense of self-worth by appreciating and supporting them genuinely. This means being nonjudgmental in conversations, not criticizing their decisions or choices and praising certain traits that they have. You can say something like - *"You are the smartest person I know. I respect how calmly and maturely you handle even the most awkward situations."*

6. Ask about their financial situation

Financial abuse is a hidden reality in toxic relationships. So, it is important that you observe how financially secure your loved one appears.

Do they lack adequate money to care for themselves?

Do they need to ask the toxic person every time before spending money?

Have they left their job recently?

While you may not be able to directly help your loved one with the finances, you can encourage them to seek legal help, support them in finding a new job or access resources provided by charities.

7. Help them be safe

While not all toxic relationships are physically abusive, domestic violence is a reality that mostly goes unreported. If you observe signs of physical abuse, encourage them to open up about their traumatic experiences. For instance, you can say -

"Hey, that looks like a really bad injury. Are you okay? Is there anything you want to tell me?"

If your loved one chooses to share about their experience, be empathetic and ask them to seek medical and legal help, if necessary.

8. Be a friend

The best thing you can do to help a friend in a toxic relationship is be supportive and just be there for them. Sometimes knowing that there's someone you can count on can make all the difference.

Be patient and don't jump into "rescue" them

While it is natural for us to rush into things and get our loved one out of the difficult situation, it is important that you do not get too personally involved or obsessed about helping them. Stay detached but concerned.

Changing Toxic Patterns of Behavior

CHRISTY PIPER

It is possible to change toxic patterns of behavior. But the prerequisite is the person must want to change. No one else can want that for them or do it for them. Change is difficult, otherwise everyone would do it. Nothing can take the place of doing the hard work to change your patterns.

Admit you hurt others

If you think you are perfect and do no wrong, you can't admit your flaws. Therefore, you can't change.

First, you'll need to silence your ego. You'll need to admit that you were wrong. That you mistreated people - whether intentionally or not. The result was that you hurt them. You need to be willing to sit with this discomfort. Feel their pain as your own.

Does it feel good to hurt those who love and care about you? Of course not. But this should give you the motivation you need to change.

Think about the type of person you admire. Decide who you want to be, and become it.

Feelings & mindset

Toxic people share a lot of common traits. They have a mindset of lack and defensiveness. They feel competitive with others and a need to control others. They speak badly about other people and think mean thoughts about them. They get jealous easily. They believe there's not enough goodness to go around, and that someone else's success takes away from their own. They spend a lot of their time feeling angry. These lead to negative thoughts.

They think they must fool people into liking them and do what they want. They are often putting on an act. They may say they believe one thing, but actually think another.

They want others to think they're a good and worthy person, but don't feel this way on the inside. The problem is, this mindset leads to unhappiness. You may fool some people with your charm for a while. But these toxic thoughts will consume you.

If you didn't realize there was something wrong with your mindset, don't beat yourself up. You were likely raised in an environment that programmed you to think this way. At the time, you didn't know any better. But as an adult, this mindset no longer serves you.

The important thing is that you now want to change, and are willing to take the steps to do it.

Changing your feelings, thoughts & character = A renewed life

Your thoughts won't change overnight. But instead of leaning in to them and letting them run wild and in the direction of negativity, you can question them. Not every thought you think is true. It is just your limited perception.

Replacing thoughts

It is not as easy as just saying, *"Stop thinking negative thoughts."* This is like someone saying, *"Don't think of a purple dancing monkey."* Sure enough, the image will pop into your mind.

When a negative thought arises, ask yourself if it's the only truth? If a negative thought or worry comes to mind, it's okay. Don't beat yourself up. There will always be a negative truth. But what you focus on in life is what you'll get more of. Just start by coming up with two positive truths to outweigh each negative one.

Repeating habits cause lasting change

A toxic person's thinking habit is a huge part of the problem. Their ingrained thinking habits are negative. One way to replace negative thoughts with positive ones is through a gratitude journal. Even writing down just three things you're grateful for once a day leads to change.

It's best to write in your gratitude journal once or twice per day. When you first wake up and right before falling asleep are the best times. This is because your mind is most impressionable and easier to program during these times.

This habit will force you to think about the good things in life, instead of the bad. Over time, seeing the positive side becomes part of your personality.

Pause and choose your words carefully

Even the words you use to describe an event can change a meaning or intention from negative to positive. Before saying words, you typically would, pause and think for a while. Ask yourself:

"How can I say this in a more gentle and positive way?"

This goes for both your self-talk and speaking with others. When you say negative and jarring statements, it can be hurtful and offensive to others. Even if you think it's clever or funny. Positive people with a healthy mindset will want to run away from you. And you'll just be left with other unhealthy people, or alone.

When you say things gently, people will love you for it. No one likes it when someone is constantly pointing out their mistakes, flaws and imperfections. Not even toxic people. When you are a pleasant person to be around, you will attract other pleasant people. You will be happier, and even like yourself more.

 Once you experience the positive results of this, you won't want to go back. Give it time. This doesn't happen overnight. Others also need time to see and trust that you've actually changed. If they felt guarded around you before, they won't change their opinion of you immediately. Patience with yourself and others s vital.

Changing yourself vs changing others

If you're hoping to change someone else, this won't work. If you treat them better after taking these steps yourself, they may slowly change their behavior towards you.

If they don't, all you can do is ask them if they're ready to change. But you'll need to watch their actions. Don't just listen to empty promises. Many abusers will say anything in the moment to keep you around. The only way you know they've changed is to watch actions over a very long period of time.

How Therapy Can Help Toxic Relationships

DR. JOSH GRESSEL

Toxic relationships are a reality. We need to be aware of toxic and abusive patterns in relationships, and know when to extricate ourselves from them. But framing the issue as something "out there" happening to me "in here" may promote a victim mentality. It may appear to be talking about a poor, defenseless person (usually a woman) who is sucked into a web of toxicity by a scheming, manipulative male. Poor you! Bad him!

The truth is far more layered. Our world cannot be so neatly divided into innocent victims and toxic perpetrators. Relationships often form between two people who share a similar emotional wound, but have different coping strategies to deal with it.

These complementary coping strategies can create a dynamic where each person tries to heal their respective wounds through the relationship.

Jack and Jill's Story

Let's make this concrete. Let's say you and your partner both were brought up in a house where you felt like you weren't enough.

- Not good enough.
- Not smart enough.
- Not pretty enough.
- Not talented enough.
- Just not enough.

Usually a woman (let's call her Jill) will cope with this wound by trying to please in relationships: *"If I'm good to you, you'll be good to me, and if you're good to me, that means I'm good enough."*

A man (let's call him Jack) with this wound will usually cope through trying to prove himself in some external way: "I drive a nice car, I make a lot of money, I have a piece of arm candy who looks up to me so that makes me good enough."

What do you think happens when Jack and Jill get together? Initially, all goes well because Jack is very intent on making a big impression on Jill - taking her out on fancy dates, treating her nicely, and acting like the perfect gentleman. Jill caters to Jack's every need, because if he loves her then she's good enough.

The problem is that these are coping strategies for both of them, and they can't weather many storms. As soon as Jill's adoring gaze is withdrawn, or as soon as Jack's gentlemanly behavior has a hiccup, there's a disruption in the symmetrical coping strategies and the core sense of "not enough" re-emerges through defensive behavior. Jill gets clingy or controlling. Jack gets cold or verbally nasty. One person's defensive behavior triggers the other, and the cycle descends into a toxic relationship.

The only way out of this is through consciousness and taking responsibility. Both sides need to become aware of the nature of their core wound and take responsibility for dealing with it, instead of hoping their partner will make it go away. It is only through competent therapy, either individually or as a couple, can both Jack and Jill can overcome their issues because if left untended, this picture won't be pretty. The problem ultimately isn't "out there" but "in here." Wholeness is an inside job.

Editor's Note

Types of therapy

Whether you are seeking therapy as a couple or as an individual, understanding the various approaches to therapy can help you better cope with your toxic relationship –

Cognitive behavioral therapy (CBT): Focuses on changing negative thoughts and behaviors.

Psychoanalytic therapy: Explores unconscious thoughts and childhood experiences to understand current behavior.

Humanistic therapy: Emphasizes self-exploration and personal growth.

Dialectical behavior therapy (DBT): Blends CBT with mindfulness techniques to manage emotions and improve relationships.

Interpersonal therapy (IPT): Focuses on improving communication and relationship skills.

Psychodynamic therapy: Explores unconscious conflicts and past experiences to understand current behavior.

Family therapy: Involves the whole family in therapy to improve communication and relationships.

Art therapy: Uses creative expression to explore emotions and facilitate healing.

Play therapy: Uses play to help children express themselves and cope with difficult emotions.

Group therapy: Involves a therapist leading a group of individuals with similar issues to provide support and guidance.

Relationship/couples therapy: Focuses on improving communication, resolving conflict, and enhancing intimacy in romantic relationships.

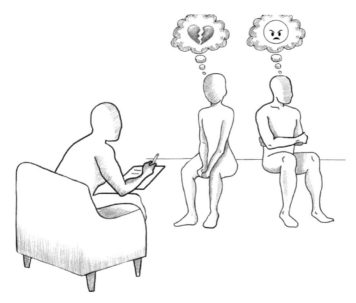

Can therapy fix your relationship?

Therapy often acts as a last resort for numerous couples in toxic relationships. Hence, relationship counseling can be a challenging, complex and time-consuming process. However, it can be very effective depending on the willingness of the parties involved. If either partner is hesitant, then it may take more time for therapy to be proven effective. But it can still help the relationship heal gradually. A therapist can help the couple set strong boundaries, be less codependent, avoid unnecessary drama, develop secure attachment styles and boost relationship satisfaction in the long run.

However, open and effective communication is a vital part of counseling and therapy as it can affect the treatment well as the outcome. Honest & positive communication can help both individuals break down their issues, establish relationship goals, provide and gain crucial feedback and heal over time.

Trying to Change a Toxic Person

JULIE L. HALL

You're reading this book because you may have loved or still love a toxic person. They may have great qualities that attracted you in the first place. They may be talented, smart, funny, or good looking. You may share the same hobbies, like the same music, or agree about politics.

It is natural to want to help that person or save the relationship, especially if they are a family member or someone with whom you have a history or children. You may tell yourself if you pushed the person to change or helped them change that things would improve. Maybe they have even made promises to change. However, the reality is that lasting change is difficult, takes time, and must be personally motivated. This is true for all of us, but especially someone with an unstable personality structure and lifelong patterns of reactivity, delusional thinking, and aggression (overt or covert).

Developmental deficits of Cluster B personalities

Cluster B personalities have profound developmental deficits that stem from attachment problems in early childhood. This means they never reached important psycho-emotional milestones and did not develop the following key features of a healthy and morally responsible personality:

- **Whole object relations and object constancy**, which enable us to understand our emotions, see ourselves and others realistically, and sustain feelings of trust and connection with others

- **Emotional empathy,** which allows us to acknowledge our vulnerability, hold compassion for ourselves and others, and respect differences in others.
- **Self-esteem,** which is a source of internal stability that enables us to manage our emotions and form trust with others.
- **Self-awareness**, which helps us see ourselves realistically and take responsibility for our actions.

Toxic personalities compensate for their deficits with -

- Delusions of victimhood or superiority;
- Denying behavior in themselves they don't wish to take responsibility for and projecting it onto others.
- Using and abusing others, often horrifically, to manage their emotions.

These coping patterns are deeply ingrained lifelong conditioned responses that feel like survival and are therefore very difficult to unlearn. Adding to the challenge is the fact that the Cluster B type, particularly the narcissist and antisocial person, has a fail-safe delusion that they are never wrong and therefore never need to change.

Like anyone, borderline, narcissistic, and sociopathic personalities are capable of change. They can educate themselves and seek professional help to build self-awareness, emotional regulation, emotional literacy, self-esteem, and trust with others. But this happens through long-term committed relational repair and self-esteem and identity development work in appropriate therapy. It is not something that can be done by a friend, partner, or family member, especially someone who has a history of overlooking and excusing abusive behavior in the Cluster B person and shielding them from consequences.

For the Cluster B type, especially the narcissist and antisocial personality, serious consequences such as incarceration or the loss of a job or a marriage are usually the only things that can motivate personal change. Even then, most do not stick with the difficult work of developing healthier patterns.

How to Make a
Toxic Relationship Work

LINDA GREYMAN

All relationships are complicated, especially if they are toxic. Sometimes due to the nature of a relationship and certain unavoidable factors, we are often unable to leave a toxic relationship, even when we want to. In such cases, it is easier to lose hope and feel trapped for eternity. However, by setting strong personal boundaries and some ground rules, you can make the toxic relationship work and protect your mental health.

Setting boundaries

1.   Identify what is acceptable or unacceptable for you
Boundaries are a form of self-care. So, you should know where you want to draw the line and where exactly you want to enforce your boundaries. Figure out which specific behaviors you consider toxic & refuse to accept. You need to understand how you get affected by such toxicity.

It is also important that you recognize your core values to understand what you will not accept in YOURSELF, such as seeking external validation and people pleasing behavior.

Identifying your boundaries will give you clarity and make it easier for you to communicate and uphold it.

2.   Clearly establish your boundaries
Once you have identified your boundaries, you need to make the toxic person aware about them. Calmly, gently, clearly but firmly communicate your needs, expectations, requirements

and boundaries. Be strict and strong, but don't be aggressive. Answer their queries but don't justify your decisions or feel guilty for having boundaries. The objective is to protect yourself, not to take revenge. For instance, you can say –

"I am not going to respond to you as long as you keep shouting and threatening me. If you want to have a calm and mature discussion, let's do it. Else I am not interested."

3. Communicate the consequences

Once you have clearly communicated your boundaries, set what consequences may follow if they are violated. Make sure the toxic person knows and understands that if they keep abusing you or refuse to respect your boundaries repeatedly, then there will be retaliation and negative outcomes for their behavior. Be clear & assertive when communicating the consequences.

For example - *"If you try to snoop on my phone without my permission one more time, I will make sure our friends and family know about your toxic behaviors."*

"If you hit me one more time, I will walk out the door and never come back. I don't deserve such abuse."

It is very important that you stand your ground and fight for your boundaries and follow through on the consequences to make sure the toxic person follows them.

4. Limit your expectations

Do not expect the toxic person to follow everything you say and become the most obedient person you have ever known. Have realistic and practical expectations as the person will probably try to reject the notion of you having boundaries and will try to violate them frequently at first. However, this is just to test how serious and strict you are about your boundaries. Be stern and strong not just about setting boundaries but also maintaining them. But be realistic and progress one step at a time.

5. Seek support

Establishing and asserting your boundaries can be challenging in a toxic relationship when you are isolated and all alone. This is why, reaching out for support from trusted loved ones, family members, friends, therapists or support groups can be extremely helpful. Support of loved ones can help you stay grounded, gain new perspectives, heal and remain assertive about your boundaries.

When your boundaries are not respected

It is highly likely that the toxic person will violate your boundaries initially as it typically takes some time to adjust to new boundaries in a toxic relationship. The reality is you cannot compel the toxic person to respect your rules and expectations. However, you can use a few steps to make sure your boundaries are not violated repeatedly in the long run.

1. Negotiate when necessary

Be open to negotiating some boundaries while being strict about the more important ones. Identify your negotiable and non-negotiable boundaries and think carefully if some can be compromised for a better future.

2. Stay vigilant

Observe and document every time a boundary is violated and how you and the toxic person have reacted or responded to it. This will help you analyze what is working and what's not and make necessary adjustments accordingly.

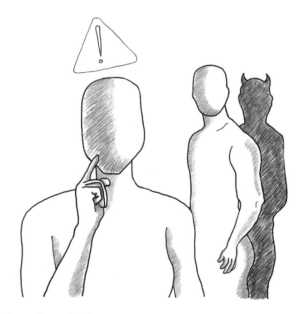

3. Stay detached

Realize that the toxic person will never fully accept your boundaries willingly. So do not be too attached to the outcome and learn to let go of minor issues. Remember your primary goal is to protect yourself and your mental health. Control your own emotions and reactions while being serious about upholding your boundaries.

Be resolute in maintaining your boundaries

Make sure that your boundaries are not minimized to empty threats without a punch. Have the determination to follow through on the consequences. However, consequences should not be about punishing or taking revenge on the toxic person. It should be about making them more compliant.

When you set and maintain your boundaries, you are putting yourself first and taking control of your life.

Chapter Six

WINGS OF FREEDOM

MOVING ON FROM A TOXIC RELATIONSHIP

How to Move Forward

KIM SAEED

One of the most severe consequences of dedicating so much energy to a narcissist is that you are left with a looming inability to enjoy your former interests and the little things that have always inspired you. You fail to value yourself and to appreciate the value in other things. Moving forward seems impossible.

Narcissists cause their victims this kind of damage. Even though it is a characteristic of their abuse, it has nothing to do with your actual worth. It is a slow attack on your beautiful spark of life and, concurrently, the toxic and inevitable effect of being involved with a narcissistic individual.

Unfortunately, the narcissist's victim is the last person in the world who is going to make the narcissist awaken to their dysfunctional and toxic behaviors. You must walk away if you are a victim because the narcissist's abuse and unreasonableness will always outlast your sanity.

Moving forward

When you're free from the narcissist's control, the world might seem strange to you. There's a good chance that you second guess every decision you make. There might be times when your behavior is more impulsive than you recall.

This is normal.

Long-term narcissistic abuse rewires critical areas of the brain. You were living in a state of fight-or-flight during your abuse. Despite the threat being gone, your brain has been trained to live in fear as its default state. But the good news is that this negative rewiring can be reversed owing to the power of neuroplasticity.

Neuroplasticity is like a superpower of the brain. It means the brain can change and get stronger when you learn and practice things, like playing an instrument or solving puzzles. Neuroplasticity can help the brain to reorganize itself and heal from injury – whether physical or emotional. This requires forming new, healing habits and avoiding those that cause us to stay in fight-or-flight mode.

The first step, if at all possible, is to remove oneself from the toxic relationship. It's nearly impossible to heal from trauma in an environment where you are constantly exposed to trauma.

The most important healing habit - 'No Contact'

A lot of times, our misery is caused by the choices we make. Humans are highly creative when it comes to denying the negative consequences of our actions. In other words, we've become so addicted to the crazy cycles we've created with a toxic person that we find just about any excuse to let them back into our lives.

But just as an alcoholic will pay the price if they give in and go on a bender, a person who violates 'No Contact' will also pay a fee.

In the event of shared custody, 'Extreme Modified Contact' should be implemented. This generally entails the use of landline and email communications, allowing cell phone communication only in emergencies or none at all, if circumstances allow.

It also means not leaving yourself (or your schedule) at the mercy of the abuser. Strict details regarding visitation and communications with your child should be incorporated into your custody agreement with the assistance of your attorney.

No Contact is not giving up on the relationship. It is deciding you deserve happiness, respect, and peace of mind. Staying in a toxic relationship that will eventually lead to your complete devastation isn't noble. "*Staying the course, no matter what*" is an archaic, dogmatic "*rule of life*" passed down through generations and perpetuates toxic relationship dynamics.

Editor's Note

What is no contact?

The No Contact rule is an effective strategy to get over a breakup or relationship dissolution. It requires you to cut off all forms of contact with a toxic person, including calls, texts, emails, social media interactions or random visits to their home.

Beyond no contact

Healing your self-image after relational harm is a continual process. Incorporate these points into your strategy for healing:

1. Surround yourself with supportive people

Reconnect with the people the narcissist forced you to leave - they'll hopefully understand. It is possible or some individuals to validate your experiences, and you can digest their positive characteristics in a healthy manner.

2. Do something the narcissist kept you from doing

Perhaps this is a hobby, a career, or something you've always wanted to do. Get in touch with your inner child and do something just because you want to. For so long, the narcissist has held you back, and now is the time to live your life according to your terms. But make sure your actions aren't motivated by spite.

3. Move forward slowly

Getting to know yourself again is part of the healing process after relational harm; it's okay not to know everything yet. Moving too quickly can lead to another toxic situation or unhealthy coping methods.

4. Set boundaries and stand your ground

To protect your well-being from abusers and manipulators, it's important to establish and enforce personal boundaries. Be assertive and stand your ground. However, it can be challenging to differentiate between healthy relationships and those that compromise your identity. Reflecting on values and seeking support can help distinguish constructive advice from negative criticism.

5. Ban, block, and cut them out

Toxic people will take advantage of any opportunity to keep you in their web. "No contact" isn't easy - especially after you were forced into dependency by your abuser - but it's the most effective path forward after the abuse.

Editor's Note

Moving forward after an abusive relationship can be a challenging and emotionally taxing journey, but it is a journey that is worth taking. It's important to acknowledge that healing is not a linear process and that it can take time, but with the right support and resources, it is achievable.

HEALING

PROGRESS

TIME

———————————— How we want healing to work

How healing actually works

Prioritizing your own safety, seeking professional therapy and support from trusted friends and family, and practicing self-care and self-compassion are all essential steps to take.

Remember that you are not alone and that there are people who care and want to help you. By taking the time to heal and rebuild your life, you can create a brighter future for yourself and experience the joy and happiness that you deserve

Living with Trauma after Moving on

KIM SAEED

Trauma results from exceptionally stressful events that shatter your sense of security and make you feel helpless in a dangerous or abusive environment. Psychological trauma can lead to persistent feelings of anxiety, upsetting emotions, and memories that don't fade away. It can also result in a sense of numbness, isolation, and inability to trust others.

Trauma often involves a threat to life or safety, but it can also occur even if you don't feel physically harmed. In the aftermath of toxic relationships, if your psychological trauma symptoms don't ease up, or if they get worse, and you find that you can't move on from the event, it may indicate that you have Post-Traumatic Stress Disorder (PTSD). Psychological shock can result from emotional trauma, but when your nervous system gets "stuck" and you cannot make sense of what happened or process your emotions, it becomes PTSD.

In addition to the challenges of relational harm, victims may also develop Stockholm Syndrome, a condition that makes it difficult to leave an abusive relationship. It's important to note, though, that not every abusive situation leads to Stockholm Syndrome

What makes narcissistic abuse different from other traumas

While there are many ways to live with trauma, living and coping after narcissistic abuse or relational harm requires a somewhat different approach than the trauma that might happen after a mugging, car accident, or natural disaster.

Unlike accidents or natural disasters, narcissistic abuse is calculated to focus like a laser beam on just this dimension of your psyche. The narcissistic abuser wants you to believe that no one cares about you, and that no one should care about you because you, as a person, are not loveable, have no redeeming qualities, and are a waste of space and time. This is probably the most significant trauma one must live with after narcissistic abuse.

Tips to live with trauma after abuse

Following are some tips on coping with your grief, healing from your trauma, and moving forward.

1. Guided meditations

Much of the material that focuses on living with trauma emphasizes the need to exercise and get moving. But what happens when you feel so destroyed that you can't get out of bed? This is where guided meditations can be beneficial. Numerous studies have shown that meditation can reduce the symptoms of PTSD, even in war veterans.

According to these studies, meditation lowers stress hormones by calming the sympathetic nervous system, which is responsible for 'fight-or-flight' responses.

Guided meditations are especially helpful for emotional abuse survivors because they allow you to focus on the narrator's voice and often use guided imagery. This differs from silent meditation, where one sits in silence and tries to manage their thoughts.

Our brains are malleable in response to trauma, and the same flexibility allows us to recover from it.

Through guided meditation, we can gain a new perspective on past experiences and change the structure of our brains, which ultimately helps us heal from trauma.

Once you gain emotional resilience, you can begin planning activities incorporating movement, such as exercise or walking in nature.

2. Don't isolate yourself

It is natural to want to withdraw from others following a traumatic event, but isolation only exacerbates the problem. Spending time with others face-to-face and maintaining relationships will help you heal.

However, don't seek support from those who invalidate what you have gone through or give you half-hearted advice on moving forward. Unless someone has experienced emotional abuse and manipulation, they won't truly understand what you have gone through.

3. You don't have to talk about the trauma

Trauma doesn't always have to be the subject of conversation when connecting with others. Some people find that this actually makes things more difficult. The feeling of being accepted for who you are is often enough to bring comfort. When you DO feel ready to talk about your traumas, it's advisable to do so with a professional, such as a therapist or coach.

Well-meaning friends and family may not validate your experience or have the knowledge needed to help you.

4. Self-regulate your nervous system

Knowing that you can calm yourself no matter how agitated, anxious, or out of control you feel is crucial. This will not only relieve trauma-related anxiety, but also give you a more positive sense of control. This can be achieved through mindful activities such as -

- Staying grounded to build a better connection with yourself and to stay calm even in uncertainty and chaos.
- Mindful breathing to stimulate the healthy function of the vagus nerve.
- Acknowledging your feelings about the trauma as they arise and accepting them, as opposed to stuffing everything down and soldiering on

It's also important to avoid activities that will shock your nervous system, such as -

- Keeping tabs on an ex through monitoring their social media
- Maintaining relationships with toxic people
- Going back through old mementos, texts, emails, and pictures

Working through trauma is often frightening, painful, and potentially re-traumatizing, so it is wise to approach this healing work delicately. You may need to spend time finding the proper support and healing modalities for you.

It can be overwhelming to live with trauma and heal from it. You have many options available to you, and if you use them, you will feel better. Keep in mind, healing is not linear, and there are many hiccups along the way. But with consistency, you will notice a difference and begin to enjoy life again.

Editor's Note

If you are suffering from chronic stress, anxiety, trauma or PTSD and if it is affecting your normal functioning, kindly consult a mental health professional or a trauma-informed therapist immediately.

How to Cope with an Intrusive Ex

DOMINIQUE INKROTT &
FORREST TALLEY

After leaving a toxic relationship, it is important to have a clean break and sever any ties that would keep you connected to your ex. This can be difficult if your ex makes efforts to push their way back into your life. This can happen after any breakup, and sometimes the intrusion is innocent - after all, if you were a good partner, your ex may understandably miss you and wish they could go back to the earlier days of your relationship.

However, when you have left a toxic relationship, your ex's intrusion in your life can be pernicious. Toxic partners will frequently disregard your boundaries and use subtle manipulation to push their way back into your life. It is important to recognize the signs of intrusion from an ex and be prepared to enforce your boundaries. You also need to be prepared to cope with the frustration and temptation that you may feel from an intrusive ex.

Tips to deal with a toxic intrusive ex

These are some healthy ways you can cope and enforce your own boundaries:

1. Know your boundaries clearly

The best approach after a breakup is "no-contact." Once you have sorted out the logistics of the breakup, there is no need for any contact with one another. Moreover, maintaining contact or communication can make it tempting to rekindle the relationship, or it may motivate you to make poor decisions like rushing into another (possibly toxic) relationship.

A clean break is your best safeguard against a post-breakup backslide, and a "no-contact" policy leaves no question about how much communication will be tolerated.

2. Resist the temptation to respond when a toxic ex reaches out

Of course, your decision to go "no-contact" does not guarantee that your ex will go along with that. Often intrusiveness starts with something that seems benign, such as a social media "like" or a generic holiday/birthday text.

But these small bids for connection can easily escalate if you respond. The simplest way to enforce boundaries in this situation is by refusing to engage or respond in any way.

3. Set safeguards by blocking and unfollowing

If your ex continues pushing your boundaries and becoming more intrusive, you need to be prepared to stand up for yourself clearly and firmly. This may mean explicitly stating your boundaries (i.e., no-contact, as in *'I will not be communicating with you any further'*), or even blocking your ex's phone number and social media accounts, etc.

4. Seek support and accountability from friends and family

Enforcing boundaries with an intrusive ex is easier said than done. Be proactive and don't leave yourself vulnerable to the distraction or comfort that your ex may provide. Talk with your friends and family about your efforts to maintain no-contact with your ex and how you will enforce that. The support and accountability of the people closest to you can be tremendously helpful.

5. Keep your mind busy and engaged

Boredom or lack of purpose can make attention from your ex seem much more enticing. Make sure your time and energy are kept purposeful by staying engaged with meaningful activities, hobbies, and projects.

Now is the perfect time to learn a new skill, spend time with family, volunteer in the community, take up a new hobby, go on a vacation, or start a side hustle. When your mind is engaged and your life is full and rewarding, an intrusive ex will be less tempting and feel easier to ignore.

6. Prioritize safety

If your ex is intrusive to the point that you are concerned for your own safety (or that of others), do not hesitate to take whatever steps are necessary to keep yourself safe.

Editor's Note

When ending a toxic relationship, prioritizing your safety becomes a crucial step, even if you are not at risk physically. Have a clear backup and exit plan to protect yourself, your loved ones and your resources, especially when your intrusive ex is adamant and vindictive. Keep local emergency contacts handy and do not hesitate to seek help from trusted loved ones.

Being prepared to deal with an intrusive, toxic ex will empower you to move on and have the confidence to build a better life for yourself with healthier relationships that you deserve.

The Dangers of Getting Back with a Toxic Ex

CHRISTINA (COMMON EGO)

There are so many dangers that come with getting back with a toxic ex. One major (and very real) danger is that the cycle of abuse could start all over again. If your ex was emotionally abusive, they might try to gaslight you or manipulate you into thinking that the abuse was your fault. They might also try to isolate you from your friends and family so that you're more reliant on them.

So why, then, do so many victims end up willingly jumping back into the cycle of abuse so often?

Why victims end up taking their abusers back

In some cases, the victim genuinely believes that the abuser has changed and that they can have a healthy relationship. Other times, the victim may be feeling insecure or lonely and believe that their abuser is the only one who truly loves them.

There's also a psychological phenomenon known as *"trauma bonding"* which can cause victims to develop an emotional attachment to their abuser. This attachment is often stronger than any other kind of bond (including familial bonds) and can cause victims to rationalize away their abuse in order to stay with the person they're attached to.

Understanding the trauma bond

The trauma bond forms as a result of intermittent reinforcement, which means that the abuser will alternate between periods of abuse and periods of "good behavior."

The victim starts to believe that the good times mean their abuser truly cares for them, when in most cases, the abuser is much more concerned with themselves.

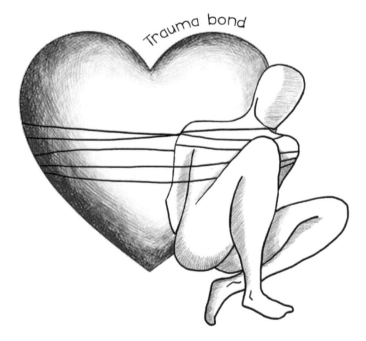

Trauma bond

Things you can lose by taking your toxic ex back

1. Your self-esteem

A relationship with a toxic ex is likely to be full of put-downs, criticisms, and other emotional abuse. This can lead to the victim doubting their own worth and believing that they deserve the abuse.

2. Your safety

If your ex was abusive in any way, there's a very real danger that they will start the cycle of abuse again. Think about what your physical and emotional health means to you before you say yes to taking your toxic ex back.

3. Your peace of mind

A toxic relationship is draining both emotionally and mentally. You might find yourself constantly worrying about what your ex is going to do or say next. If you're not in a good place mentally, it's going to be very difficult for you to have a healthy and happy relationship with anyone – including yourself.

What to do if you've already taken your toxic ex back

If you've already taken your ex back, it's important to be honest with yourself about the dangers of staying in the relationship. If your ex was abusive, there is a very real possibility that they will manipulate and abuse you again.

It's also important to reach out to your friends and family members as they can support you, remind you of your worth and encourage you to stay safe. There are also many domestic violence hotlines which can offer advice and resources if you're feeling unsafe or trapped in your relationship.

Protecting Yourself
from a Vindictive Ex

KAYTEE GILLIS, LCSW

Breakups happen to most of us, and they are rarely pleasant. Anger, frustration, and pain are among some of the many difficult emotions often experienced during a breakup from a romantic partnership.

Unfortunately, some people feel wronged, and even vindictive, during the ending of a relationship. These individuals do not know what to do with the pain and discomfort they are experiencing, and feel they need to seek revenge towards their ex for causing them this pain.

Many toxic people, especially if they lack empathy, will see you ending the relationship as a direct insult to them. The tighter the perpetrator feels tethered to the relationship, the more invested they will be in lashing out and seeking revenge. This is often why, when a victim leaves, this is considered the most dangerous time for them. Not just physically, but socially, professionally, and financially you could be at risk.

Tips to protect yourself from your ex

Once their efforts to win you back have failed, your toxic ex will only lash out worse, taking revenge, as they most likely feel you have damaged their ego. They might think –

"How dare they leave me?"

"Who do they think they are?"

Do not think that physical abuse is the limit: socially, professionally, and financially their victims are at risk. Your

301

friends, your job, and your money are all potential weapons to an abusive ex-partner. Please take your safety seriously. It is better to be wrong and feel silly than right and risk serious harm or even death.

These steps will help you protect yourself when a vindictive ex is out for revenge:

1. Protect all living things first and foremost

If you have shared children, unfortunately, they might become a weapon used against you after a breakup. Ensure their safety throughout. Do not hide from your children that you and your partner are separating, and make it clear that it is not their fault. Seek legal support if minor children are involved, specifically from someone experienced in domestic violence.

Without these qualifications, even a highly skilled and well-meaning professional can fail to see the signs and dangers of leaving an abusive situation. Therefore, take the time to seek out specialists related to your case. Do this sooner than later.

2. Change all locks on doors, and lock all windows

Consider getting a security camera if financially able to do so, even if only for the front door. In extreme cases, if possible, move to a safer location or a new apartment that your ex is not aware of. Staying somewhere safe is crucial for your physical safety and for your mental health.

3. Protect meaningful or sentimental personal belongings

Take care to protect the items that mean the most to you, such as your children's baby pictures or your grandmother's necklace. Protect items that your partner knows to be of value to you. Unfortunately, someone who is out for revenge will look for these things that they know mean a lot to you in order to seek revenge.

4. Protect technology

Change all of your passwords on everything, even if you recently changed them. Change lock screens, banking passwords, email, and social media. Remember that they know you and your habits, so change all or your personality. If you usually have your child's name or birthday as your password, choose something random like "water3981".

5. Shut off any access to finances

Prevent their access to your credit cards and bank accounts, if you are legally able to do this. If you are married, seek legal advice to see what you can do to best protect yourself. If they were listed with authorized access to any bank accounts, inform these entities in writing that you revoke this access. Remove them from all your work paperwork or as beneficiaries to all savings accounts, 401k, IRA, etc. If possible, take cash out of the bank and put it in a safe place.

Betty, a 45-year-old woman from Colorado, did not remove her ex from her credit cards upon the breakup. She took his word that he would not charge them during the breakup. He ended up maxing them out, and left her with over 20k in debt.

6. Gather copies of all important documents

Make sure to take hold of all necessary documents like passports, deeds to the house, medical documents, etc. Take originals if they legally belong to you, copies if they are jointly owned. Do not trust that a toxic person will do the honest thing and provide you with paperwork that you need. Protect yourself.

7. Protect your career and professional reputation

Consider telling employers and coworkers that your ex is angry and out for revenge. Many people do not tell others outside of their immediate social circle what is going on because they want to keep things private, and because it can be extremely embarrassing to deal with this sort of situation. But a vindictive ex will think nothing of calling your employer to make trouble, or even coming to your place of employment. You want to stay one step ahead of them.

8. Do not try to convince others of your side of the story

If someone seems to be playing both sides, such as mutual friends, cut ties with them. It does not have to be forever. If friends do not want to choose sides, choose for them in a respectful way:

"I need to take some time for myself right now and distance myself from Sally because her behavior is scaring me. Thank you for understanding".

9. Seek legal protection

If you have proof of their harassment and retaliation, especially if it has turned threatening or physical, consider seeking a protection order. The laws in support of this will be different in every state and country, so seek legal advice on the best course of action. We know that a protection order cannot stop someone who is out to harm you, but it can give you the protection you need to feel safer and more confident when you need to enlist support such as calling the police.

10. Build a support system

Lastly, an important feature of your safety plan is the importance of building support. Begin to open up to friends about your concerns and fears regarding your safety after ending the relationship. Countless victims typically avoid sharing any of their fears with others for as long as they could because they were embarrassed about what was going on. Your safety is not worth this. Decrease the amount of isolation, and do not suffer in silence.

Join a support group, even if online. Seek the support of a therapist or coach who specializes in post separation abuse.

Remember, even with a safety plan in place, you may not be able to cover all possible outcomes, so remain prepared, keep your emergency numbers available, and seek support.

Seeking Closure

JULIE L. HALL

Seeking closure is a natural response to a traumatic experience. We look for understanding, meaning, and a sense of finality so we can release the painful hold the trauma has on us and move on. But achieving a sense of resolution about a toxic relationship is tricky territory. Depending on how you see closure, it can help you heal, or it can keep you stuck in self-defeating cycles.

Unhealthy ideas about closure

Here are common but unrealistic and dangerous ideas about closure with a narcissist.

1. I need to get the narcissist to see my point of view.

You've been trying to get them to see your perspective throughout the relationship, and threatening to leave or leaving isn't going to make it happen either, even if they make promises to do it. The toxic personality is myopically self-focused and lacks the empathy needed to consider or care about your feelings and needs.

2. I need the narcissist to admit they are wrong.

Admitting to wrong and backing it up by taking responsibility violates narcissists' basic personal code that they are never to blame and always justified. You may as well expect a turtle to give up its shell.

3. I need to confront the narcissist about their narcissism.

It may be therapeutic for you to confront the toxic person, but most of the time it isn't productive and could lead to further harm for you. Make sure you're prepared for them reacting negatively. Telling a narcissist about their narcissism usually elicits rage and/or them projecting it back onto you by telling you (and others) that you're the narcissist.

4.   I need the narcissist to change.

Narcissists can change, but it is unusual and takes personal commitment, time, and a great deal of hard work. Their biggest obstacle is that whenever they have an interpersonal problem, they experience emotional splitting, which makes them shut down self-reflection and externalize blame onto others. You become the enemy, and effective communication becomes impossible.

5.   I need others to acknowledge the narcissist's abuse.

It is important to get validation for the abuse you have experienced, but you need to be realistic about who you seek it from. Others in your family or social circle may have their own relationship with the narcissist and forms of denial about the narcissist and themselves that make it difficult for them to see the situation clearly. Society in general has collective denial about narcissistic abuse, particularly parental narcissistic abuse, which can lead to judgment or bad advice for the victim. Even many therapists do not understand personality disorders and their traumatizing impact on others.

Healthy closure

Wanting the narcissist to see your perspective and take responsibility is fair and understandable. So is wanting other people in your circle to acknowledge the abuse and support you. But expecting these things to happen and making your recovery contingent on them will only keep you stuck. You can't control these things. What you do have control over is you.

Continue to educate yourself, seek validation from others who understand, and work on your self-awareness, emotional literacy, and self-esteem. Closure is for you and about you. You will feel it when you no longer need to focus on processing the trauma and can look to healthier and happier times ahead.

Can Spirituality Help Survive the Trauma?

KIM SAEED

Spirituality is a powerful tool for helping individuals overcome the trauma of narcissistic abuse. Trauma is any experience that is emotionally or physically painful and can often leave individuals feeling overwhelmed, powerless, and lost. Finding ways to heal and cope with the emotional pain that narcissistic abuse can cause is essential for a person's well-being and overall mental health.

Can spirituality heal trauma?

One-way individuals can work through the trauma of narcissistic abuse is through spiritual practices. Spirituality is a belief in and connection to something greater than oneself. It is a way of finding meaning and purpose in life and developing a sense of connectedness to a higher power.

By engaging in spiritual practices, survivors can find peace and hope in their lives. Through prayer, meditation, and reflection, survivors can better understand their emotions and how to manage them. These practices can also provide comfort and strength in the midst of difficult times, allowing survivors to remain grounded and centered.

In addition to providing emotional comfort and strength, spirituality can help people gain perspective on their trauma. Spiritual practices enable individuals to make sense of their trauma and move forward in their lives. Survivors may benefit from this perspective when developing a plan for dealing with trauma and eventually moving on.

Editor's Note

How spirituality can help

Spirituality helps you connect with your inner self. It gives you the courage to sit with your pain, accept your reality and find hope in the fact that the universe is guiding you towards a better future. It makes you see the bigger picture and realize that your suffering and trauma is making you stronger and a better individual.

Here are some ways that spirituality can help you overcome trauma:

1. Finding meaning and purpose

Spiritual practices can help us understand and find meaning out of traumatic experiences. For example, you may find comfort in the belief that your suffering has a purpose or that it is part of a larger plan.

2. Learning to cope better

Many spiritual practices, such as meditation and prayer, can be used as coping strategies that can help you manage symptoms of trauma, such as anxiety, depression, and hypervigilance.

3. A sense of support

Spirituality can provide a sense of community and belonging, which can be particularly important for abuse and trauma survivors. Being part of a supportive spiritual community can provide a sense of safety and connectedness that can help you feel less isolated and alone.

4. Forgiveness and healing

Spiritual practices can help you cultivate forgiveness and compassion, both for yourself and for others. This
can be an important part of the healing process, allowing you to let go of feelings of anger, bitterness, and resentment and move towards a place of healing and wholeness.

Five Spiritual practices to overcome trauma

Trauma can manifest itself in many ways, sometimes for years after the traumatic event has passed. It can be challenging to move forward and heal from the experience, but there are spiritual activities that can help. Here are some examples of how to use spirituality to overcome trauma.

1. Guided meditation

Guided meditation can be a powerful tool to help you heal from trauma. You can focus on healing your body, mind, and spirit in guided meditation. You can use them to visualize yourself in a safe and peaceful place, release negative energy or thoughts, and accept and forgive yourself and any other people involved. It's important to note that forgiveness is not always necessary to move on. Some people find the notion of forced forgiveness to be toxic. Toxic forgiveness is a type of forgiveness that is motivated by a need to please or control someone else rather than a genuine desire to heal or move on. It often involves suppressing one's true feelings and allowing the other person to get away with harmful behavior. Toxic forgiveness can lead to further resentment and emotional harm.

2. Journaling

Journaling is a great way to work through any emotions that come up as a result of trauma. Writing can be cathartic, and it can help you to express and process your thoughts and feelings. You can also journal about any spiritual experiences or insights that arise as you process your recovery from narcissistic abuse.

3. Yoga

Yoga can be an effective way to reduce stress and find inner peace. It can help to balance your body and mind, and can be an excellent tool for connecting with yourself and your spirit.

4. Reiki

Reiki is a form of energy healing that can heal emotional and physical trauma. It works by balancing the body's energy and creating a state of relaxation. Reiki can help reduce stress, anxiety, and depression and help with physical pain. It can help heal trauma by releasing stored emotional energy, allowing the body to heal itself. Reiki can help to reduce the intensity of the trauma, allowing the person to process the experience in a healthier way.

5. Pranic healing

Pranic healing is another form of energy healing that uses prana, or life force energy, to heal physical and emotional ailments. It is believed that when trauma is experienced, the energy in our body gets blocked and causes physical, mental, and emotional imbalances.

Pranic healing helps to unblock the energy and restore balance in the body. Pranic healing is a non-invasive, gentle technique that can help heal emotional trauma. Practitioners use a combination of breathing exercises, meditation, and visualization to help clear and balance the energy in the body, as well as to bring awareness to the areas of the body that need healing.

Pranic healing also helps to reduce pain, improve sleep, and reduce stress levels.

Spirituality and healing

Spirituality can provide individuals with a sense of community and support. By engaging in spiritual practices, individuals can connect with others who are also dealing with similar issues and find strength in shared experiences. This can be especially beneficial for those dealing with the trauma of narcissistic abuse, as it can provide a safe space for survivors to talk about their experiences and gain support from others.

Overall, spirituality can be a powerful tool for helping survivors to cope with and overcome the trauma of toxic relationships,

Rebuilding Yourself with Self-Love & Self-Care

SIGNE M. HEGESTAND

It ought to be pretty straightforward to show yourself love and kindness, but it is not as easy especially if you have been the victim of abuse, since it is designed to destroy you and your "self". It is vital that you separate yourself from your critical and degrading thoughts and start developing a more loving, caring, acknowledging and respectful inner voice.

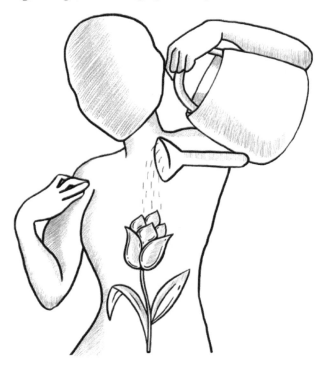

Editor's Note

What is self-love?

Love for self is caring about your own wellbeing & happiness. It refers to appreciating your own worth, meeting your needs and refusing to compromise on your values to please others. Unlike selfishness or narcissism, self-love is a necessity and can boost our self-confidence, self-esteem and sense of self.

What is self-care?

Self-care is the process of trying to improve and protect your own wellbeing and happiness, especially during difficult times. It involves prioritizing your physical and mental health, avoiding unhealthy coping mechanisms and engaging in daily self-care habits like exercising, getting enough sleep and eating healthy.

Practicing Self-love

Self-love and self-care are not about "just" getting a massage or buying something for yourself. It is about the way you are in touch with yourself. Self-compassion contains several elements, such as -

- You have to acknowledge your suffering as you would in another person.
- When you display compassion, you are affected by the suffering and feel it inside. You must relate to the painful aspects with understanding and kindness.
- Last, but not least, compassion contains an acknowledgement that suffering, failure and imperfection are feelings all people encounter.

You recognize that you have been through something painful

and perhaps even abusive or violent. Your experiences might have led to feelings of being unloved, wrong or perhaps even unworthy. You might be ashamed, or feel guilty.

Try sensing it in your body. Where does the suffering or emotion stem from? Maybe your throat or chest feels constricted. Allow these sensations to unfold and meet yourself with kindness and empathy. For instance, you may tell yourself -

"I understand that this is painful and difficult, it has been hard and I understand why I am sad, or angry."

Different emotions might arise when you allow yourself to feel your suffering. Others would feel the same if they had been through what you have. You might say that you are creating the same loving, safe and caring relationship as if you were to comfort someone else.

Acknowledging emotions

Maybe you are thinking that this will only make things worse, that you may get stuck in difficult emotions. But in practice it is the opposite. By acknowledging your emotional reactions, which are healthy and natural responses to what you have been through, your nervous system is strengthened and soothed.

Remember that emotions are "just" emotions, they are neither good nor bad, they just are. It is human to sense and feel what you feel, and it serves as your personal signal, like an inner compass you can use to navigate from. In this case, you need to take it seriously.

Your compass might not point due north after being in a relationship where you were told your emotional experiences were wrong or that you were 'too' sensitive, which may have caused you to doubt yourself. This was always a part of your partner's way to gain power and control over you.

You need to reclaim yourself and your emotions. They are a central part of improving your ability to establish boundaries, since your emotions tell you what you like/don't like or if you should say yes or no. Anger is an emotion that helps you stop something, or move you away from situations/people that are not good for or respectful to you.

Strategies to practice self-love

Incorporating simple daily practices can help you prioritize yourself and cultivate a sense of self-compassion. One effective practice is to set aside even just 5 minutes a day to focus on yourself.

Breathing techniques are also a valuable tool for supporting your process of liberation and restoration.

These techniques can have a positive effect on your nervous system, which may be strained from your past experiences. Additionally, they can be used as a form of self-reassurance. A good beginner exercise is to simply notice your breathing as it is right now.

Another powerful practice is to start a daily gratitude journal. This will help you acknowledge even the smallest things that bring you joy in your daily life. Be detailed in your descriptions as this will help your brain focus on the positive instead of automatically reverting to negative thoughts. Aim to write down 3-5 positive things each day.

To be loving in your relationship with yourself is paramount for your journey to return to who you truly are and to reclaim your life.

Editor's Note

How to love yourself when you've been abused?

Loving yourself can be very challenging when you have been in a toxic environment longer than you should have been. However, self-love and self-care can empower us to reconnect with our inner self and find happiness once again. Here's how you can get started on the journey of loving yourself and healing-

1. Accept yourself as you are in all your flawed glory. Instead of believing the criticisms of your abuser, accept that you are imperfect like everyone else and work on improving yourself.

2. Do not blame yourself for what you have experienced and endured. You did not provoke the toxic person to be abusive. That's just the way they are.

3. Forgive yourself for being in a toxic relationship for this long and not being able to leave. Forgive yourself for doing what you thought was right. Forgive yourself for being afraid of abuse, for being insecure, codependent and afraid.

4. Choose to believe your thoughts, perceptions, feelings and experiences, not the lies of the toxic person. Your thoughts are valid. Don't give in to gaslighting.

5. Forgive yourself for being hopeful. For hoping the toxic person would change someday and love you for who you are. Forgive yourself for being in love with someone who only wanted to hurt you.

6. Be empathetic, kind and compassionate with yourself. Be mindful about your self-talk and treat yourself like you would treat a friend in a toxic relationship be understanding, helpful and loving.

7. Celebrate yourself and everything about you, your failures, efforts and achievements. Reward yourself for the genuine efforts you put in to achieve your goals.

Importance of self-love in healing from abuse

Self-love, self-care and self-compassion can feel selfish and wrong when you have been manipulated and abused. However, once you leave the toxic environment, you need to realize how important it is for you to love yourself unconditionally and accept yourself as you are in order to heal.

Self-love makes us realize that we are worth being happy and gives us the strength to reject anything less. It helps us improve our self-esteem that has been ravaged by abuse. It can also make us feel more resilient, optimistic, in control of our emotions and enable us to better cope with internal conflicts. Self-love can help us heal from trauma, anxiety, panic attacks and the feeling of walking on eggshells all the time.

Self-love helps to counter the dehumanizing effects of abuse and makes us believe, once again, that we are worthy. That we deserve to be loved and respected.

Learning to be in a
Healthy Relationship

CHRISTY PIPER

A toxic relationship can scar people for life. There is no doubt about that. After a traumatic experience in a toxic relationship, many people fear trying a relationship with another person. It's easy to think any other relationship will turn out the same, as if there's no way to prevent it.

But this is unfounded fear, as long as you can learn how to trust your intuition. Your intuition was likely stifled and confused by toxic people in your past. You did not know how to see the signs of an unsafe person. But this instinct can be re-learned at any age.

Take time to heal before dating again

It's not smart to jump into another relationship soon after leaving a toxic one. It almost never ends well. Most people find a similar or worse partner. So don't base your judgment off these experiences. If you haven't put in the time and effort to change, the people you attract will be the same.

When you change yourself and raise your standards, you will feel different. If you are a different person, you will attract different people - both in your platonic AND romantic relationships.

Recognizing and honoring your inner guidance system

Now that you see and know what you did not like about your past toxic relationships, you have a huge advantage. Not every toxic relationship is the same. But chances are, a lot of the times you wanted to say no to something, you didn't. Either you said yes to please them, or were talked into doing it. You were made to feel insignificant as if your feelings or thoughts did not matter.

There were little things you felt were wrong, but you went along with the toxic person anyway. They likely had a strong energy and a way of convincing you to do things their way. Know that your feelings are valid. If your new date attempts to stifle or minimize your view, trust this to be a red flag.

If you start to feel these emotions again, and feel forced into doing things your new partner's way, this is a sign to either talk about it or get out. Getting out without communicating about it is at your discretion. If you feel the person is way out of line with no hope of being healthy, you can simply tell them you don't think it's working out.

If you think there was a misunderstanding or they didn't mean to dismiss you, you can ask them about it. Do not pour the details of your past toxic relationships onto them. Avoid accusing them of anything, which will put anyone on the defense. It's a good idea to simply say how their actions or words are making you feel. If they make no efforts to apologize or correct it, just know that's a big sign they could be toxic.

Recognize that triggers don't mean your new partner is toxic

When you find a new, good partner, don't think that they won't trigger you at all. Even the most innocent acts from a healthy person can trigger someone who has been stomped on by toxic people. They may do something that reminds you of someone toxic in your past. But remember their intention may be totally different.

A healthy partner can help you work through these triggers. When a trigger comes up, identify what it feels like for you. Recognize why you were triggered. Try to link it to a past event that it reminded you of. Now notice why it's different this time.

Work on your triggers by telling another person

Importance of telling your partner what you're thinking & feeling

It's important to tell your partner what's going on if you start feeling very triggered. Pinpointing the issue early can help save a lot of misunderstandings and heartache.

They'll be able to express themselves differently and explain their intentions. It is likely different than what the trigger made you feel. This way you can remap and heal this trigger in your mind. Eventually, you'll stop reacting negatively to it.

Sandra's Story

Sandra had experienced toxic relationships with three different partners in the past, each showing their true nature after a few weeks or months of being together. She would go from very happy, to utterly sad and crying all the time. This left her feeling disappointed and unhappy, and she didn't want to repeat the same pattern. So, she waited three years before moving in with Jim, her current partner, despite having moved in quickly with her past partners.

However, even though Jim had shown no signs of being toxic, Sandra felt trapped and scared after moving in with him. She couldn't shake off the fear that she experienced in her past relationships.

It wasn't until she confided in someone and spoke about her fear aloud that she was able to get past it. By addressing her trigger and realizing that Jim was nothing like her past partners, she was able to relax and enjoy her relationship with him.

Sandra's story highlights the impact that past experiences can have on our present relationships. It also shows how seeking help and talking through our fears can be instrumental in overcoming them.

Mindset: From lack & fear to love & winning together

In your past toxic relationships, you probably felt fearful to voice your true opinions. You got punished a lot for little to no reason. You didn't know if your partner would be mad at you when they came home. There were a lot of needless ups and downs. This confuses your nervous system.

A toxic person thinks by using fear tactics, they can control you. This comes from a place of lack. It's important to realize that a healthy partner has a totally different mindset. They know that when you are both happy, this is a win-win. They know that when they bring you up, their spirit is lifted, too. They do little things to make you happy. They don't keep you feeling confused and fearful.

Even when a healthy partner criticizes you, they do it to genuinely help you improve. Not just to be mean. There's also a good chance they will provide suggestions that can help you improve. Not just hurl insults to make you feel bad. You won't fear communicating your thoughts and feelings to a healthy partner. If you do fear it, is it founded or unfounded fear?

Ask yourself if your past is the reason for your fear. Strong communication is absolutely necessary to build a healthy and solid relationship.

Be aware of your own toxic behaviors & take ownership

Know that spending so much time around a past toxic partner still affects you. The bad habits you learned, the way you fought back, and the triggers you reacted to do not go away overnight. So be mindful of bringing these into your new relationship.

Believing a healthy partner is trying to hurt you won't have good results. How you act can either bring out the best or worst in your new partner- just like it did in you.

Know that ultimately, you are the one responsible for any toxic behaviors and reactions you bring into your new relationship. Your partner can help you. But they are not responsible for correcting them. Don't place this burden on them too much. It comes across as needy, which may have them treating you like a child or helpless person.

Remember that you want to be equal adults in a healthy relationship. You do not want to drag in issues from any past relationships if possible. You don't want to feel like their charity project. You don't want them to feel sorry for you. These things will make them start to lose attraction for you. If a healthy relationship is your goal, treat your partner as you want them to treat you.

When the past creates problems in the present

Problems can arise when two partners with toxic exes come together. But this is actually quite common. There is a lot of past pain you can both relate to. Just realize you can easily trigger each other, and it can devolve into disrespect. In this case, try to be the bigger person. Especially, if you are the more evolved one, which is likely because you're reading this book.

Say aloud that you should stop arguing. If your partner continues, say you're leaving to calm down and walk away. It's not helpful to keep feeding into each other's anger.

Be forgiving, as you want them to be with you. If they make mistakes, give them the chance to correct it. In your heart, you'll know if they are genuinely trying to improve. If you feel like it's not enough, tell them. Say how much you love and care about them, but that you need to see more improvement. Make sure you are putting in genuine effort, too.

See less of them if possible. This can give them a chance to reset and notice their mistakes. They'll realize how much they miss and appreciate you. They will realize you're a priority in their life, and don't want to lose you. If a partner is healthy, they will come back showing changed behavior in the long run.

Repeat these steps as often as you need to. Improvement and becoming healthy is an ongoing process. But with effort on your part, a loving relationship with a healthy partner is very possible and rewarding. A healthy relationship is even sweeter after experiencing a toxic relationship.

The Bigger Picture

DARLENE LANCER

Ending a toxic relationship requires growth, courage, and support. It's not the end of the story, however, but a step toward recovery. We still may have regret, grief, loneliness, guilt, shame, resentment, PTSD, and ingrained codependent habits.

We've suffered losses: lost time, confidence, and relationships. Fear of loss can make us avoid new relationships that leave us alone. It's easy to cling to our wounds and feel like a victim. These signs indicate there's work to be done.

It's important to look at the big picture

Abuse and trauma are passed on generationally and beyond our control and comprehension. But we can focus on our recovery and learn to live an authentic, self-directed, soul-centered life.

Full recovery holds many gifts:

- We gain self-knowledge and learn to honor and express our feelings, needs, and wants.
- We learn to set boundaries and no longer tolerate disrespectful behavior.
- We reclaim ourselves and individuate from our families. This is a life process, and many people don't achieve it, but trauma pushes us to forge our own identity.
- We gain compassion for others and for ourselves.
- The entire focus of our lives can change. We may

initiate a new career or move to a new city.

- We take responsibility for our own happiness.
- Our self-esteem no longer depends on other people.
- We have greater autonomy.
- We're capable of intimacy.
- With healthy self-esteem, we experience our own power.
- Untethered from our past, we feel expansive and creative.
- We have energy to pursue our passions.
- We may renew or discover a spiritual relationship with a higher power.
- We develop fulfilling, healthy, reciprocal new relationships.
- Rather than react to other people, we follow our internal cues - our guidance system - and trust ourselves.
- We're able to identify, nurture, and comfort ourselves so that we're not drawn to unhealthy relationships.

Leaving a toxic relationship is no small feat. Remember that the courage you found will help you create a new life.

AUTHORS

 ### Angel J. Storm, Ph.D.

Dr. Angel Storm - a certified life coach holds a Ph.D. in Conflict Analysis and Resolution with a concentration in International Peace, an M.A. in International Security, and a B.S. in Human Development. She served in the US Army for six years and continued work for the Defence Department for another seven years as a civilian. After her own experience in family court with a narcissist in 2017, she began life coaching and focusing on narcissistic abuse recovery. She loves helping people in all stages of narcissistic abuse recovery get their lives on track and grow in their purpose, despite having all the cards stacked against them.

Website: https://bio.site/the_manifold_mind

 ### Beverly D. Flaxington

Beverly is a three-time Amazon bestselling and Gold-award winning author. Her books include "Understanding Other People: The Five Secrets to Human Behavior", which won the gold award from Readers Favorite. She is an entrepreneur, adjunct professor at Suffolk University and a well-known international speaker on many topics related to human behavior and relationships.

Website: https://the-collaborative.com/

Christy Piper

Hi, my name is Christy and I help women and men heal after a toxic relationship so that they can find a great partner. Why would I want to do that? I discovered my passion after seeing how people who are vulnerable to toxic relationships get taken advantage of in a lot of different areas of their life.

Website: https://www.christypiper.com/

Christina (Common Ego)

Through her weekly YouTube videos, personalized coaching, and transformative self-development programs, Christina sparks hope within survivors, helping them to recognize and break free from abusive partners and embrace a life of resilience and empowerment. For more information visit commonego.com and unlock the path to healing and self-discovery.

Website: https://commonego.com/

Darlene Lancer, JD, LMFT

A prominent relationship expert and media spokesperson, Darlene Lancer is a marriage and family therapist who has counselled individuals and couples internationally for over 30 years. She's the author of 10 books, including Codependency for Dummies, Dating, Loving, and Leaving a Narcissist: Essential Tools for Improving or Leaving Narcissistic and Abusive

Relationships, and Conquering Shame and Codependency: 8 Steps to Freeing the True You. Follow her popular blog and receive a free copy of "14 Tips for Letting Go" at

Website: https://whatiscodependency.com

 ### Dominique Inkrott, LSW

Dominique Inkrott is a Licensed Social Worker. She completed her Master of Social Work in 2018, and has worked with a variety of populations in various settings - VA hospitals, private medical centers, and multiple counselling centers. She has chosen to focus her work on couples and relationship issues, a clinical focus which has been very rewarding. She also writes a blog and hosts a podcast exploring dating, relationships, and related issues facing young adult women.

Website: https://quitkissingfrogs.com/

 ### Forrest Talley, Ph.D.

Dr. Forrest Talley is a clinical psychologist who has worked in a variety of settings (as a Co-Training Director of an APA internship, primary supervisor, Army psychologist, college professor, and psychologically informed janitor). He currently has a private practice and can be contacted at **Website:** https://forresttalley.com/

Elinor Greenberg, Ph.D.

Dr. Elinor Greenberg, Ph.D., is a psychologist and internationally renowned Gestalt therapy trainer who specializes in the diagnosis and treatment of Borderline, Narcissistic, and Schizoid adaptations. Dr. Greenberg is the author of the book: Borderline, Narcissistic, and Schizoid Adaptations: The Pursuit of Love, Admiration, and Safety.

Website: http://elinorgreenberg.com/

Jesston Williams

Jesston Williams has worked in various capacities in the health and financial sectors for many years. He is currently the Executive Director of Tangelic. With Tangelic, Jesston works to build and implement tactics to achieve strategic goals and collaborates with non-profit organizations to create state-wide plans for poverty alleviation. Jesston is also a board member with Fund for Empowerment, a Phoenix, Arizona-based non-profit organization whose mission is to build community resources for oppressed and marginalized people via direct services, capacity-building training, and project support. When he's not leading the day-to-day operations of Tangelic, Jesston enjoys writing. He is the author of "In the Eye of the Father: A Memoir of Faith and Redemption.

Website: http://tangeliclife.org/

Josh Gressel, Ph.D.

Dr. Josh Gressel is a licensed clinical psychologist with over 35 years of experience, practicing in the San Francisco Bay Area. He practices using sand tray therapy, is a Certified Imago Therapist, and currently is in a certification program for Ketamine-assisted therapy.

Website: https://www.joshgressel.com/

Julie L. Hall

Contributions by Julie L. Hall, author of The Narcissist in Your Life: Recognizing the Patterns and Learning to Break Free, Hachette Books, founder of NarcissistFamilyFiles.com, and international speaker and trauma coach.

Website: https://narcissistfamilyfiles.com/

Kristin Davin, Psy.D.

Dr. Kristin Davin is a Licensed Psychologist with over 17 years of experience. She specializes in working with individuals to improve how they manage conflict, learn healthy modes of communication, gain valuable tools for overcoming codependent and unhealthy relationship patterns, and find a deeper connection to themselves. She takes a collaborative approach to therapy and coaching centered around meeting each person where they are, tailoring sessions to their unique path of growth and purpose.

Website: https://reflectionsfromacrossthecouch.com/

Kim Saeed

Known for her best-selling writing and renowned coaching, Kim Saeed lives in Virginia. For the past 10 years, she has coached thousands of people and offered consulting services to therapists and mental health professionals. Her specialties include relationships, breakups, and narcissistic personalities.

Website: https://kimsaeed.com/

Kaytee Gillis, LCSW-BACS

Kaytee is a psychotherapist and writer who specializes in working with survivors of traumatic relationships. Her recent book, Invisible Bruises: How a Better Understanding of the Patterns of Domestic Violence Can Help Survivors Navigate the Legal System sheds light on the ways that the legal system can perpetuate the cycle of domestic violence by failing to recognize IPV patterns.

Website: https://www.kaytlyngillislcsw.com/

Mariette Jansen, Ph.D.

Dr. Mariette Jansen is a narcissism relationship expert and life coach, who has written two self-help books: From Victim to Victor and Rulebook of a Narcissist. Both are available via Amazon.

Website https://drdestress.co.uk/

Peg O'Connor, Ph.D.

Dr. Peg O'Connor is the author of Higher and Friendly Powers: Transforming Addiction and Suffering (Wild house Publications, 2022) and Life on the Rocks: Finding Meaning in Addiction and Recovery (Central Recovery Press, 2016).

Website: https://pegoconnorauthor.com/

Signe M. Hegestand

Signe M. Hege stand (b.1974) Licensed Clinical Psychologist, Author, Psychotherapist, and TEDx speaker 2019. She specializes in working with victims of psychological abuse and other dysfunctional relations.

Website: https://www.hegestand.dk/en

GLOSSARY OF TERMS

Abuse

It refers to any behavior or action meant to intentionally hurt, injure or harm another individual. Abuse can be physical, sexual, emotional, verbal, psychological or financial. It is meant to manipulate, control, intimidate, frighten, threaten or hurt someone.

ADHD/Attention-Deficit Hyperactivity Disorder

A neurodevelopmental disorder of childhood, ADHD is characterized by inattention and/or hyperactivity impulsivity which can affect one's ability to function even in adulthood.

Adverse Childhood Experiences (ACES)

It refers to possible traumatic experiences and events, such as abuse, neglect or violence that are experienced by a child between the ages of 0-17.

Altruism

It refers to one's selfless concern and consequent action to promote the well-being of others even at a cost to themselves.

Antisocial Personality Disorder

Also known as sociopathy, it is marked by disregard of the needs or rights of others. People with this disorder are typically deceitful, reckless, irresponsible, manipulative and prone to engage in criminal behavior.

Attachment Styles

According to the attachment theory in psychology, attachment styles refer to the attitudes and behavioral patterns one shows in relationships. It shows how we relate to intimate partners based on how we were attached to our parents as children. Four types of attachment styles are observed in adults - secure attachment, anxious attachment, avoidant attachment, and fearful-avoidant (or disorganized) attachment.

Authoritarian Leadership Style

It is a leadership style where the focus is primarily on centralized authority, dominance, and control over others, especially subordinates. The goal is to gain unquestioning obedience.

Avoidant Attachment Style

When a primary caregiver doesn't appropriately respond to a child's needs beyond providing basic necessities like food & shelter, the child can develop an avoidant attachment. As adults, they are fiercely independent, feel sad or anxious and feel uncomfortable with intimacy.

Blame Shifting

It refers to the act of deflecting responsibility for one's actions onto another person or external circumstances, often to accepting their own faults, and to avoid accountability or negative consequences.

Borderline Personality Disorder (BPD)

Borderline personality disorder is a psychological condition involving extreme mood swings, difficulty managing emotions, and unstable behavior and relationships. People with BPD are highly prone to self-destructive behavior & suicide.

Burnout

It refers to a physical, mental and emotional state of exhaustion developed due to extreme and prolonged stress. It is often caused by chronic workplace, household or relational stress.

Codependency

It is a psychological condition where a person is overly reliant on another, neglecting their own needs and well-being. Also known as relationship addiction, codependent relationships are typically abusive, emotionally destructive and lack boundaries.

Coercion

The act of convincing or compelling someone to do something involuntarily using force or threats.

Cognitive Impairment

It refers to problems with one's ability to think, remember, learn new information, concentrate, make decisions or use their judgment which adversely affects their daily life.

Closure

It refers to the process of accepting and resolving emotions related to the end of a romantic relationship in order to move forward and heal emotionally.

Cluster B Personality Disorders

These are mental disorders which affect one's thoughts, emotions & behaviors causing actions that are unpredictable, erratic, dramatic, attention-seeking and overly emotional. There are 4 types of Cluster B personality disorders - antisocial, borderline, histrionic and narcissistic personality disorder.

Complex PTSD/CPTSD

It is a psychological conditional where the sufferer experiences the symptoms of PTSD and some additional symptoms, like trouble managing emotions, distrustfulness, uncontrollable anger etc.

Conduct Disorder

A type of behavior disorder, it refers to antisocial behavior in children. The child may be irresponsible or disregard social norms & rules.

Control by Proxy

It refers to a situation where one person controls or manipulates others' behaviors and actions through a third party, such as friends, family members etc.

Coping Mechanism

A psychological strategy that allows one to adapt to environmental stress, whether consciously or unconsciously, to reduce tension, gain better control over self & experience psychological comfort in a stressful situation.

Dark Triad Personality

It refers to offensive personality traits involving narcissism, psychopathy and Machiavellianism - separate but related personality types. People with these traits are charming yet toxic.

Delusion

It is a belief that a person believes to be real or true or real when in reality it is false. The delusional person may keep believing in their delusion despite evidence proving the contrary. It is a symptom of different psychological conditions.

Dementia

It is a clinical syndrome characterized by a general cognitive decline, such as impaired ability to think or memory loss that can negatively affect a person's ability to independently perform daily activities.

Developmental Delays

It occurs when development in a child delays, stops, slows or reverses and the child fails to reach developmental milestones as expected or as compared to other children of the same age.

Domestic Violence

Also known as intimate partner violence, it refers to negative, harmful and abusive behavior patterns used to control and gain power over an intimate partner. Domestic violence can also be experienced by other immediate family members in a domestic circle.

Eating Disorders

It is the disruption in one's eating behavior with a strong focus on their body weight that can negatively affect their psychosocial functioning and physical health. It can present as severe psychiatric illnesses.

Emotional Detachment

It is our unwillingness or incapability to connect with or relate to others emotionally. It can help someone avoid unnecessary stress, anxiety and drama.

Empathy

It is the ability to sense, relate to and share the feelings of others. Empathy allows us to understand what someone else is thinking or feeling.

Empath

It refers to people who are highly perceptive of the thoughts and emotions of others due to some intuitive capabilities. They have difficulty setting boundaries and absorb others' energies easily.

Enabling/Enabler

A form of codependency, enabling occurs when an individual acts as rescuer, savior or caretaker to enable another person to act and behave in toxic, negative and destructive ways. Enablers encourage loved ones to continue their toxic behavior by denying or ignoring their toxicity and by trying to "fix" them.

Epigenetic Changes

Epigenetics refers to the study of how our behaviors and environment can lead to changes which can alter how our genes work. Epigenetic changes refer to genetic modifications which influence gene activity without making any changes to the DNA sequence.

External Validation

In psychology, it refers to the process of seeking external confirmation or approval from others to validate one's own emotions, thoughts, self-worth or identity, often as a means of reducing anxiety or self-doubt.

Fail-Safe Delusion

It refers to a belief that, regardless of what happens, one's personal beliefs and worldview is correct, and hence, any contradictory evidence is typically ignored.

Fight/Flight Response

Also known as the fight-flight-freeze response, it is a natural physiological response to a perceived harmful, frightening or stressful experience or event. It helps the body to fight or run when faced with a threat.

Flying Monkeys

It refers to individuals recruited by a narcissist or other

manipulative person to act as their enablers, defenders or attack dogs. Flying monkeys do the abuser's bidding without question and gather information on their behalf.

Frustration Attraction

It refers to the phenomenon where feelings of frustration or uncertainty can intensify attraction to a partner or potential partner. The increased effort required to obtain your potential or existing partner's attention can heighten your attraction towards them.

Gaslighting

A psychological manipulation strategy, gaslighting is used by an abuser to make their victim doubt themselves, and question their own memories, judgment, sanity & reality.

Histrionic Personality Disorder

It is a psychological condition marked by inappropriate & attention-seeking behavior. Someone with this disorder may have unstable emotions, behave dramatically, be extremely enthusiastic, have a distorted self-image yet be highly charming.

Hypervigilance

It refers to a state of constantly elevated alertness for analyzing potential threats in the environment. Hypervigilance is often caused by trauma.

Insecure Attachment

A pattern of attachment in intimate relationships where one partner feels insecure and worried about their bonding, closeness and intimacy with the other partner.

Intermittent Reinforcement

It is a form of psychological abuse involving a pattern of rewards (affection) at irregular intervals mixed with random bursts of abusive behavior. It is done to control the victim and to make them more obedient.

Internal Validation

In psychology, it refers to the process of self-affirmation and self-acceptance, based on one's own values, beliefs, and experiences, without relying on external sources for validation or approval.

Intimate Partner Violence

It is a form of domestic violence carried out on a former or existing intimate partner or spouse by an abusive current or former partner. It can include physical, sexual, verbal, emotional and financial abuse.

Intuition

It is the instinctive ability to gain knowledge immediately without the use or need for conscious reasoning.

Jekyll and Hyde Personality

Based on Robert Louis Stevenson's popular novel The Strange Case of Dr. Jekyll and Mr. Hyde, it refers to someone with a dual personality of which one is honest and good but the other is harmful and evil. The person alternates between the dual personalities, which are separate and opposite.

Love-Bombing

It is a manipulation strategy used to influence and control a person by giving them excessive attention, affection and admiration. It is used to charm someone and gain their attention and affection. This is one of the initial stages in the cycle of abuse.

Love Language

It refers to how an individual prefers to express love to and receive love from their partner, such as through words of affirmation, quality time, gifts, acts of service, or physical touch.

Machiavellianism

It is a personality trait marked by an exploitative, manipulative, cynical, callous and attitude towards people. People with this personality often lack empathy, and are cynical, deceptive and cunning.

Maltreatment

It refers to intentional or unintentional harm or neglect of a person, typically a child, by a caregiver or authority figure, causing physical or emotional damage.

Mirroring

In a relationship, mirroring refers to subconsciously or consciously matching and imitating the mindset, attitude, body language, expressions, and tone of voice of the other person.

Mood Disorders

It refers to a group of mental health conditions that are marked by persistent mood disturbances. The affected person's mood or emotional state gets distorted and impairs their daily functioning.

Name-Calling

It refers to the act of using insulting or derogatory words to criticize, describe, humiliate or address someone. It is a form of verbal abuse.

Narcissism/Narcissistic Personality Disorder (NPD)

Narcissism is a personality trait characterized by having an unrealistic sense of self-importance, strong need for attention and a lack of empathy. Narcissism can also be a part of Narcissistic Personality Disorder (NPD), a mental health condition, as narcissism lies on a spectrum.

Narcissistic Abuse Syndrome/Narcissistic Victim Syndrome

It refers to negative psychological and emotional outcomes that occur when someone experiences the effects of narcissistic abuse and manipulation. It is not medically identified as a mental health condition.

Narcissistic Wound/Narcissistic Injury

It is not about what the victim has experienced. Rather, narcissistic wound refers to what an individual with narcissistic traits may experience when they are criticized, neglected, controlled, rejected, abandoned etc. It refers to the narcissist's wounded "ego".

Neuroplasticity

It refers to the brain's ability to adapt & reorganize itself by forming new neural connections in response to new experiences, learning, trauma or injury.

Neuroticism

It is a trait disposition that determines the degree to which one may experience negative emotions, such as stress, anger, irritability, depression, anxiety, emotional instability etc.

Oppositional Defiant Disorder

A form of behavior disorder in children, it is characterized by disobedient, uncooperative and defiant behavior from a child towards authority figures, such as parents & teachers.

Panic Attacks

It refers to sudden and intense episodes of fear or distress, characterized by physical symptoms such as rapid heartbeat, sweating, trembling, and shortness of breath.

Paranoia

It refers to an individual's unwarranted & unjustified belief, mistrust or suspicion that they are being threatened, betrayed, harassed or persecuted by others without having any real evidence. When it becomes intense, it can be a symptom of mental illness.

Passive Aggressive Behavior

It refers to a tendency to express negative emotions, such as anger, indirectly rather than expressing them openly. It is characterized by avoidance of direct communication and passive hostility.

People-Pleasing Behavior

It refers to a pattern of behavior in which an individual prioritizes the needs and desires of others over their own, often at the expense of their well-being.

Personality Disorder

It is a form of mental health condition where the affected person develops unhealthy & rigid patterns of thoughts, behaviors, personality, attitude and functioning. They have difficulty relating to others.

Post-Traumatic Stress Disorder (PTSD)

It is a psychological condition involving persistent mental & emotional stress developing due to a terrifying experience or event, psychological shock or physical injury.

Power Dynamics

It refers to how power is distributed in a relationship and involves the different ways both partners behave to control one another.

Psychological Aggression

Using words and behavior to control, insult, humiliate, threaten, intimidate, criticize and isolate someone, mostly a loved one.

Psychopathy

Psychopathy or sociopathy refers to a neuropsychiatric disorder. It is characterized by a lack of emotional responses, remorse & empathy, inability to form meaningful relationships, poor behavioral controls, and inability to learn from experience.

Psychopath

A psychopath is a person with psychopathic traits. They may be dishonest, impulsive, exploitative, disinhibited, antisocial, manipulative and lack empathy.

Relational Ethics

It refers to ethics within interpersonal relationships. It involves mutual respect, support, trust, acceptance and respectful engagement.

Relationship Dynamic

It refers to the existing patterns of behavior, communication and interaction between individuals in a relationship. It can include power dynamics, communication styles, and emotional & behavioral responses to each other.

Savior Complex

It refers to a state of mind where a person strongly believes they are responsible for helping or saving someone even at the cost of their own well-being. It is also known as messiah complex, white knight syndrome and Christ complex.

Schizoid Personality Disorder (SPD)

An uncommon personality disorder where someone expresses limited emotions and avoids social interactions and activities. They don't seek or enjoy close intimate relationships and are emotionally detached.

Sexual Coercion

When someone is compelled, manipulated, forced or threatened in a nonphysical way to engage in unwanted or unsolicited sexual activity.

Silent Treatment

It is an act of completely ignoring someone and being stubborn about refusing to talk to them after a disagreement or argument. It is an abusive controlling behavior to express disapproval.

Smear Campaign

A form of abuse, it is an effort to discredit, devalue, or damage the victim and their social reputation through negative propaganda and false or misleading information, such as spreading rumors or lies.

Social Anxiety

It is an intense and constant fear of being observed and judged negatively in a social setting. This can affect one's ability to build relationships.

Social Isolation

It refers to the lack of social connections and not having enough people around to interact with on a daily basis. It can cause feelings of loneliness.

Splitting

It is a defense mechanism where a person sees things as either all good or all bad. It allows one to accept and tolerate overwhelming & difficult emotions by perceiving someone as devalued or idealized. It is "characterized by two contrary and independent attitudes," according to psychoanalyst Sigmund Freud.

Stockholm Syndrome

It refers to a psychological response where abuse victims (or hostages) develop a positive bond with their abusers (or captors) as a means of coping with their trauma.

Substance Use

Substance use disorders refers to continued use or misuse of recreational drugs, nicotine, alcohol, over-the-counter drugs & other illicit substances that negatively affect the person.

Sympathetic Nervous System

It is a part of the autonomic nervous system that activates the body's fight or flight response during stress or danger.

Therapy/Psychotherapy

Therapy or psychotherapy is a form of treatment that utilizes psychological tactics and methods to help patients overcome mental disorders such as anxiety, depression and trauma.

Trauma

It is a lasting, adverse emotional response to a distressing experience or event. Experiencing a traumatic event can lead to unpredictable emotions, shock, denial, psychological illnesses, physical symptoms, difficult relationships etc.

Trauma Bonding

It is a natural response to abuse where the victim develops an unhealthy emotional connection with their abuser. It can occur in both romantic and non-romantic relationships.

Triangulation

A manipulation tactic used by toxic people to bring a third person into their toxic relationship dynamic to create a new conflict or to divert the attention from the original problem to stay in control.

Triggers

In psychology, triggers refer to stimuli or events that elicit strong emotional or behavioral reactions due to their association with past traumatic experiences or learned associations.

GLOSSARY OF TERMS

Twin Flame

A twin flame refers to an intense soul connection between two individuals. It is believed that people who are twin flames share the same soul. Hence, when twin flames meet, it can lead to a deep connection and intense attraction. A twin flame can simply be considered as an individual's "other half".

Victim Mentality / Victim Mindset

It is a personality trait that develops when a person believes themselves to be a victim of negative circumstances, outcomes and actions by others. They believe that such outcomes are not their fault even in the presence of contrary evidence.

Walk on eggshells

It means to be extremely careful and cautious about one's words, behaviors and actions to avoid upsetting, disappointing or offending someone else.

Connect with

The Minds Journal

Where the mind speaks. The heart shares. And the soul confides.

At **The Minds Journal**, we believe in the transformative power of words. Our platform brings together a collective of brilliant minds, gifted authors, and passionate experts who pour their hearts onto the canvas of thought, weaving profound narratives that resonate with the human experience. Each article, blog, poem, and artwork is crafted with meticulous care, aiming to touch the core of your being, to ignite dormant passions, and to ignite the sparks of inspiration within.

Welcome to The Minds Journal, where words unite, and souls ignite.

Our authentic, soul-stirring content supports and inspires millions of loyal followers worldwide to read, share, assess & improve. As we believe in the power of sharing perspectives and experiences, we encourage our readers to contribute their own articles, blogs, and stories which are published online as a part of our Readers' Blog.

Being strong believers in the transformative power of words, we are committed to fostering self-awareness and personal transformation through our innovative publications. Our first publication "Soul Works: The Minds Journal Collection" helped readers seek solace in the pages that delved into the realms of self-improvement, relationships and spirituality.

And now, The Minds Journal, your haven of enlightenment and connection, is proud to present this groundbreaking publication to promote awareness about toxic relationships, foster personal transformation and healing from emotional turmoil.

Connect with
The Minds Journal

But as healing knows no bounds - so doesn't The Minds Journal.

If you have faced challenges head-on, if you've navigated the complexities of toxic relationships and emotional struggles, then an extraordinary opportunity awaits for you.

We're here as a guiding companion, leading you towards something truly meaningful –

Discover a wealth of free goodies, resources and invaluable insights, guiding you through conquering toxic relationships and emerging from adversity even stronger.

At The Minds Journal, we understand the importance of healing and growth, which is why we are excited to offer you exclusive access to these empowering materials. Simply scan the QR code provided, and start your journey towards healing and self-actualization. Gain insights, strategies, and tools to navigate toxic relationships and overcome the aftermath of trauma.

Join our vibrant community of seekers, dreamers, and thinkers as we embark on a shared journey of self-awareness and personal growth. Let the words flow through you, intertwining with your thoughts and emotions, as you discover the profound beauty and strength that lies within.

Don't miss out on this opportunity to access our free goodies and resources. Scan the QR code now and let the healing begin by embarking on a life-changing adventure of self-discovery

To know more, visit us at themindsjournal.com

Printed in Poland
by Amazon Fulfillment
Poland Sp. z o.o., Wrocław